PALACE PLAYS

By the Same Author

ECHO DE PARIS

ANGELS AND MINISTERS

DETHRONEMENTS

CORNERED POETS

ODD PAIRS

IRONICAL TALES

TRIMBLERIGG

UNCLE TOM PUDD

THE LIFE OF H.R.H. THE DUKE OF FLAMBOROUGH

ALL-FELLOWS AND THE CLOAK OF FRIENDSHIP

MOONSHINE AND CLOVER

A DOORWAY IN FAIRYLAND

PALACE PLAYS

BY

LAURENCE HOUSMAN

JONATHAN CAPE
THIRTY BEDFORD SQUARE
LONDON

FIRST PUBLISHED 1930

JONATHAN CAPE LTD., 30 BEDFORD SQUARE, LONDON
AND 91 WELLINGTON STREET WEST, TORONTO
JONATHAN CAPE & HARRISON SMITH INC.
139 EAST 46TH STREET, NEW YORK

PRINTED IN GREAT BRITAIN BY J. AND J. GRAY, EDINBURGH
PAPER MADE BY JOHN DICKINSON AND CO. LTD.
BOUND BY A. W. BAIN AND CO. LTD.

Contents

Preface

TWENTY years ago I wrote and published a play called *Pains and Penalties*, the aim of which was to throw a kindly light on the character and conduct of Queen Caroline, wife of George IV. The events there recorded had happened ninety years before; but the play was banned, theatrical production was forbidden to it; and in spite of repeated application to the licensing authority, no indication was vouchsafed of any offending passage, the removal of which would enable a public performance to be given.

For thirteen years my property, as a stage-play, was destroyed. Then, when greater fish were being released from unclean aspersion (*The Cenci*, and *Mrs. Warren's Profession* amongst others) I applied again, and was told that if I would cut out the word 'adultery' – altering the sentence from 'if I ever did commit adultery' to 'if I ever did *that thing*' – and would also omit a sentence of twelve words, which I have again used in one of the following plays (page 37), the right of stage-performance should be restored to me whenever a theatrical management offered production.

The face-saving condition imposed was foolish enough, in all conscience; but why it was not made thirteen years earlier was not explained. 'In England's green and pleasant land,' it seems that a man's property can be destroyed and restored to him again, by official fiat,

9

as arbitrarily as in Soviet Russia; but, being done by a court official, it is not regarded as either dishonest or revolutionary.

I am now publishing two other plays, to one of which the Censor would probably make objection – not because of obscene passages, but because of its subject. Queen Victoria is still too sacred a character to be allowed upon the stage; and though the historic fact, that Lord Melbourne only consented to her marriage with Prince Albert on discovering that he was not her cousin, may be stated in print; and though from Mr. Strachey we learn of her own discovery of the too friendly relations of her mother, the Duchess of Kent, with one of the gentlemen of her court, these good materials for drama may not yet take appropriate form before the public eye.

But had I chosen to submit the second of these two plays – a satire on Royalty of a hundred years ago, as bitter as I could make it – its fictional element would probably have enabled it to pass, in spite of the grossness of character and action which it necessarily portrays. And satire though it be – a work of fiction, not of history – Queen Victoria is nevertheless the unseen heroine, whose understudy, Princess Augusta, makes virtue victorious. For it was mainly Queen Victoria who saved Royalty from the depths of degradation into which it had descended during the Regency and after. And so, taken together, these two plays – the one based on fact, the other mere fiction – represent two stages in our national history, the one a step up from the other. And it is Queen Victoria who, in her cool, precise way, takes the desirable step, inaugurating, by her own courageous revolt, that Vic-

torian age which made revolt (among women) so unfashion-
able. Revolt led into it, and revolt came out of it. Queen
Victoria was opposed to votes for women; but in her own
escape from leading-strings the movement had begun.

L. H.

The Revolting Daughter

The Revolting Daughter

SCENE I

The chamber is lofty but not large; its proportions, windows, doors, furniture, all suggest that it has larger connections than its floorspace alone would indicate. This often happens to the smaller apartments of great houses; proportionate breadth denied, height is thrust upon them by the architectural design of the main building. The result here is a spindly pretentiousness, modified by age; for the hangings, once splendid, are faded and shabby; the crimson carpet is worn, and the red of the curtains has had its day. In the centre of this too aspiring chamber sits a young maiden, fair and of fresh complexion; submissive in attitude, diminutive in stature, she seems nevertheless a figure of more importance than the large lady her companion, who, deferentially strict, sits directing her studies. The GOVERNESS *has at her side a small table; on it lie books and needlework. Her pupil occupies an upright chair with gilt legs, too high to be comfortable; upright as the chair she sits, straight and symmetrical, holding a book in both hands.*

GOVERNESS You have read enough for to-day, Princess. Begin your recitation.

B

(She takes a book from the table, opens it at a marked page; and the PRINCESS, *who has watched her with waiting eye, receives the signal to begin.)*

PRINCESS 'Hope deferred maketh the heart sick: but when the desire cometh it is a tree of life.

'Whoso despiseth the word shall be destroyed: but he that feareth the commandments shall be rewarded.

'The law of the wise is a fountain of life to depart from . . .'

GOVERNESS No, Princess, no! After the word 'life' there is a pause. Say it again!

PRINCESS 'The law of the wise is a fountain of life. . . . To depart from the snares of death.'

GOVERNESS You see — it makes a difference!

PRINCESS 'A wicked messenger falleth into mischief: but a faithful ambassador is health.

'Poverty and shame shall be to him that refuseth instruction: but he that regardeth reproof shall be honoured.'

(The door opens; a lady of stiff dignity enters. GOVERNESS *and pupil rise and curtsy; for this is H.R.H. the* DUCHESS OF KENT; *and though a widow of restricted means, she holds her narrow court with a rigour of decorum that requires everything. The* DUCHESS *seats herself, and by a gesture indicates that the others may sit also. She and the* GOVERNESS *both speak with a foreign accent.)*

DUCHESS What were you doing?

GOVERNESS The Princess was reciting her Scripture, Madam.

DUCHESS Continue.

PRINCESS 'He that walketh with wise men shall be wise: but a companion of fools shall be destroyed.
'A good man leaveth an inheritance to his children's children: and the wealth of the sinner is laid up for the just.'

DUCHESS My dear, sit up, and sit straight!

PRINCESS I *was* sitting straight, Mama!

DUCHESS Never answer your Mother, my dear!

> (*The* PRINCESS *struggles with her emotions. Habit is powerful: she controls herself.*)

GOVERNESS Go on, Princess.

PRINCESS 'He that spareth the rod spoileth the child: but he that loveth him chasteneth him betimes.
'The righteous eateth to the satisfying of his soul: but the belly of the wicked shall want.'

DUCHESS Lehzen! The Princess should not have been permitted to learn *that*!

GOVERNESS It's in the Bible, Madam.

DUCHESS There are things *in* the Bible, as well as out of it, which are not seemly on the lips of a young girl. . . . I hope you do not allow the Princess to read *all* the Bible?

GOVERNESS There are parts of it I do not read myself, Madam.

DUCHESS Very proper of you, I'm sure. Victoria, bring me your diary.

(*The* PRINCESS *does so; her Mother turns the pages.*)

DUCHESS When did you write in it last?

PRINCESS This morning, Mama.

DUCHESS You have not put the date. Nor have you entered the fault for which I corrected you yesterday. Go and do it at once.

PRINCESS Which fault, Mama?

DUCHESS *Which!*

PRINCESS There were so many!

DUCHESS My dear, that is almost like answering me again! Do you pretend not to remember how, when I questioned you about certain things, you lost your temper? . . . Do not lose it again *now!*

PRINCESS No, Mama.

DUCHESS There, take it to the table. . . . Mind! Do not leave anything out!

PRINCESS No, Mama.

(*The* PRINCESS *goes to a table near the window and begins writing.*)

DUCHESS Lehzen!

GOVERNESS Madam?

(*By a gesture the* DUCHESS *draws her toward her for a confidential exchange of words.*)

DUCHESS You have the history lesson prepared, as I told you?

20

GOVERNESS Yes, Madam.

DUCHESS You have marked the passage? You have put in it – the – ?

GOVERNESS Yes, Madam.

DUCHESS You are sure that you have made it *quite plain*?

GOVERNESS Yes, Madam. I have numbered the names of all heirs to the succession in order, and have underlined them in red ink. Under the Princess's name I have made *three* underlinings.

DUCHESS That is as I wished it. . . . Have you heard how the King is to-day?

GOVERNESS No, Madam.

DUCHESS They never let *me* know anything – that they can help.

GOVERNESS I heard yesterday that he was a little better. He had taken a good turn, they said.

DUCHESS They told *me* that yesterday – to annoy me. It was not true.

GOVERNESS Indeed, Madam? Then your Royal Highness has had news?

DUCHESS I have means of information about which *they* know nothing.

GOVERNESS That is very fortunate, Madam.

DUCHESS It is not a question of *fortune*. It is the respect that is due to me. They seem to forget that some day *I* shall be the Queen-Mother.

GOVERNESS They will soon find themselves reminded, Madam.

DUCHESS They will. Victoria, have you done?

PRINCESS Yes, Mama.

DUCHESS Read it!

PRINCESS Yesterday, at breakfast, after the Chaplain had read prayers, Mama said to me, 'Victoria, did you fold up your night-gown?' 'Yes, Mama,' I said. 'Did you clean your teeth?' Mama then inquired. 'Yes, Mama,' I said. Her next inquiry –

DUCHESS '*Mama's* next inquiry.' Alter it!

(*The* PRINCESS *makes the alteration.*)

PRINCESS Mama's next inquiry was whether I had said my prayers. I answered, 'You know quite well that I said them, Mama; for you were there!' My dear Mama told me not to answer like that; and I lost my temper. This was wrong of me. Mama then kindly explained that she asked all these questions – not because *she* wanted to know, but in order to get me into the habit of asking them of myself: which I always do.

DUCHESS Those last three words had better be erased. If true, it is unnecessary to say so. If not true, they sound a little like defiance.

PRINCESS They *are* true! Why mayn't I write the truth?

DUCHESS The truth, when it means answering your Mother defiantly, is not a suitable weapon in the mouth of a young girl. . . . Not another word, Victoria! You will now do your history lesson.

> (SIR JOHN CONROY, *the Duchess's major-domo, enters and comes confidentially towards her. He brings her a letter.*)

Ah, my good Sir John, so you have returned. You have news for me?

CONROY A letter, Madam. It has just come.

> (*He hands it.*)

DUCHESS Ah! I will see you again, when the Princess has finished her lessons – alone.

> (*In the last word there is an implied intimacy of understanding.* SIR JOHN *goes: he looks back; she is looking at him. Their eyes meet. Yes, there is an understanding between them. Meanwhile the* GOVERNESS *has begun the history lesson.*)

GOVERNESS We were reading yesterday, you will remember, Princess, about the House of Hanover. Why was it so called?

PRINCESS It was so called because my three-times great grandfather came over to conquer England for the Protestant faith.

GOVERNESS Not exactly to *conquer* it, Princess. He was called constitutionally, to establish the Protestant succession, and keep out all Papist pretenders.

PRINCESS Are *all* Papists pretenders?

23

GOVERNESS Yes, Princess. No Papist can sit on the throne of Great Britain.

PRINCESS Or Ireland?

GOVERNESS Or Ireland.

PRINCESS The Irish are pretenders too, aren't they?

GOVERNESS 'Are they not' – not 'aren't they. . . .' They are Papists and rebellious – a very troublesome and disagreeable people.

PRINCESS Then I need not like the Irish, need I?

GOVERNESS Only those who live in the north, in Ulster. They are industrious, and loyal, and deserving. For the rest you can have only pity.

PRINCESS And try to convert them?

GOVERNESS *Pray* for their conversion, Princess. That is all you can do.

PRINCESS I will do so to-night.

DUCHESS The dear King is worse, much worse, they tell me. Victoria, you must remember to pray to-night that his precious life may be spared. That is far more important than the conversion of the Irish. I do not think they would ever make good Protestants.

PRINCESS Very well, Mama.

GOVERNESS Begin your reading, Princess: page 273.

PRINCESS (*opening the book*) Oh, what is this?

GOVERNESS That is a chronological table, Princess, showing the succession to the crown at the present day.

24

PRINCESS Oh, how interesting! I have never seen this before. Am I in it?

GOVERNESS Your Royal Highness's name is there — with others.

PRINCESS What is the red ink for?

GOVERNESS That is to show, Princess, the order of inheritance, in the last — and in the present generation.

PRINCESS I see my Father's name.

GOVERNESS Yes, Princess. Had your Royal Father lived, he would now have been heir-presumptive to the throne.

PRINCESS Why 'presumptive'?

GOVERNESS On the presumption that His Majesty the King has no children.

PRINCESS Oh, but Cousin George told me the other day that he's had lots.

(*There is a moment of painful embarrassment. Then the* DUCHESS *speaks.*)

DUCHESS They have all died, or have passed from the succession in other ways.

PRINCESS (*a little puzzled*) Oh? . . . Then it would have been my Father?

GOVERNESS Undoubtedly.

DUCHESS (*consequentially*) Of course it would have been your Father, my dear! And *I* should have been Queen.

PRINCESS (*genuinely astonished*) La! Mama! How you surprise me! . . . Then now it is one of my uncles?

25

DUCHESS (*with asperity*) *None* of your uncles, Victoria. They do not come in, I'm thankful to say.

PRINCESS Then ... do *I*?

DUCHESS You have the table there, my dear. Study it.

PRINCESS (*after further examination*) Oh! Oh! I didn't know ... I never thought I was quite – quite – so near as that. Oh, Mama, Mama!

DUCHESS What is it, my dear? It is nothing to be upset about.

PRINCESS Oh, now I know why you have always been – so – so – Oh, I will be good! I will be good!

DUCHESS Indeed I hope so! For that a great deal depends on *both of us*. It has been *my* care hitherto. In the future it will have to be yours.

PRINCESS Oh, Mama, forgive me if I have ever – ever seemed – ungrateful! I am so young for it!

DUCHESS I shall always be there, my love. You will be Queen. But I am your Mother. I shall not go away and leave you.

PRINCESS Oh? ... No, of course not.

(*Disappointed, she weeps.*)

DUCHESS (*soothingly*) Of course not.

GOVERNESS Why, of course not, Princess. There, there! Don't cry!

DUCHESS Let her cry, Lehzen! It will be good for her. After all it's only natural; a great shock. It was time she had it.

PRINCESS It's so sudden!

DUCHESS Not as sudden as it might have been. Considering his age, the King must have a very strong constitution. It is wonderful how it has lasted. So now I must go and see after my black, to be ready in case anything happens.

GOVERNESS Is the last news very alarming, Madam?

DUCHESS Every one had given up hope yesterday, they tell me. And now he has given it up himself.

PRINCESS Is he conscious, Mama?

DUCHESS No, not conscious, my dear. He has given that up too. Perhaps that is as well. I fear he did not lead a good life.

PRINCESS But he was *married*, Mama!

(*This causes shock.*)

DUCHESS My dear! All married people do not lead a good life – not all.

PRINCESS Oh, I thought they did!

DUCHESS Victoria, you shock me! Who has been talking to you?

PRINCESS Talking to me?

DUCHESS Yes, about marriage, and – and things of *that* sort.

PRINCESS No one . . . only Cousin George. The other day he asked me to marry him. He said it would make him good.

27

DUCHESS Your Cousin George!

PRINCESS Yes; he said that all my uncles wished it, and the King wished it too. So that was why he asked me.

DUCHESS Yes. I daresay they do . . . I daresay they do! But I can tell them *this* – and I tell you too – you are not going to marry your Cousin *George*. *He is* not going to be King.

PRINCESS No, Mama, not if I am to be Queen.

DUCHESS Kiss me, my dear! Ah, you do not know the dangers from which I have protected you. I hope that you will never have to know. . . . That will do, Lehzen, for the present. You may go. The Princess will finish her lessons later.

(LEHZEN *curtsies and retires.*)

My child, listen to me! It's time that you knew – *this* at least. Ever since you were born, I have been fighting a battle to save you from the hands of *wicked men*.

PRINCESS Oh, Mama!

DUCHESS Yes. They wanted to get hold of you; but I would not let them. They wanted to choose a husband for you – your Cousin George, and then to make *him* King instead of you. But I saw what they were after. I saved you from *that*. That is why I never left you alone – never let you go out of my sight, except sometimes when we were at Windsor, and it could not be helped. That is when your Cousin George spoke to you, I suppose? . . . What did you say to him?

28

PRINCESS Of course, I said he must first ask Mama!

DUCHESS My own darling child!

PRINCESS And that didn't seem to please him.

DUCHESS No, I daresay not!

PRINCESS He said that in that case it was 'all up'!

DUCHESS That is the sort of language I should expect from him! – 'All up!' He has been learning English from his uncles – and other things as well, I'll be bound! So marrying you was going to make him *good*, was it? . . . Oh, my darling, now that you see from what I have saved you, I only ask you to remember, and be a little grateful. You are so young, so inexperienced – and such a child! But I know, oh, I know *things*! . . . But Mama is still with you, my child; always will be with you. Trust Mama! Come to Mama about *everything*!

> (*The* PRINCESS *stands dutifully attentive, wistful, interested, a little alarmed, and yet self-possessed; and when the* DUCHESS *at last pauses for her to speak, it is a portent of coming events that she does not say, 'Yes, Mama,' as perhaps she was expected to do; but stands looking out – into the future. The door opens.* SIR JOHN CONROY *enters, and stands looking at mother and daughter.*)

DUCHESS Go, now, for your walk with Lehzen.

> (*The* PRINCESS *curtsies and retires.* SIR JOHN *holds open the door, shuts it, and advances toward*

the DUCHESS. *Oh, yes, there is an understanding between them. She puts out her hand, and he takes it.*)

SCENE II

It is still dark; for in the entrance hall of Kensington Palace the shutters have not yet been unclosed. Behind a wide archway at centre burns a dim light: there is the staircase lobby. To the left of the archway one sees the foot of the stairs.

In the dark emptiness goes the clanging of a bell, followed by knocks. A FOOTMAN, *not quite dressed as he should be, enters carrying a light. He crosses from left to right, and passes out of view. You hear unchaining and unbolting of a door; then, indistinctly, voices, which grow louder as the visitors enter and become visible. Heavily cloaked,* LORD CONYNGHAM *comes in, followed by the* ARCHBISHOP.

CONYNGHAM Tell them to take the message at once! Say the matter is urgent.

FOOTMAN Yes, my Lord. But Her Royal Highness isn't up yet, my Lord.

CONYNGHAM 'Up?' Of course she's not up at this hour! Send Her Royal Highness's maid to call her.

> (*The* FOOTMAN, *having the only candle, is busy now lighting others. But the urgency of his lordship stops the business half-way; and only one set of candles gets lighted before he goes.*)

FOOTMAN Yes, my Lord.

CONYNGHAM And say His Grace the Archbishop of Canterbury, and Lord Conyngham are here to see Her Royal Highness on important business.

FOOTMAN Yes, my Lord.

CONYNGHAM Hurry, man! Hurry!

FOOTMAN Yes, my Lord; but I'll have to call the maid first.

CONYNGHAM Well, call her!

FOOTMAN Yes, my Lord; but the maids sleep where I'm not supposed to go; and the door up to it is locked. I shall have to throw up at the window.

CONYNGHAM Isn't there a bell?

FOOTMAN Yes, my Lord; in Her Royal Highness the Duchess's room there is a bell.

CONYNGHAM Well go and ask that it may be rung!

FOOTMAN (*aghast*) I daren't go to Her Royal Highness the Duchess's room, my Lord: not now. Her Royal Highness the Princess is there too.

CONYNGHAM Well, go and do the best you can. But say Her Royal Highness *must* come —

FOOTMAN Yes, my Lord.

(*Exit* FOOTMAN.)

CONYNGHAM (*finishing his sentence*) — at once! . . . Good Lord! What a house! Sleeps with the old Cat, does she?

ARCHBISHOP (*corrective, but suave*) I beg your pardon?

CONYNGHAM I – I beg yours! Yes; I suppose one oughtn't to say that now. But your Grace knows that the Duchess has been a difficulty all along.

ARCHBISHOP The Duchess is a determined character.

CONYNGHAM Yes.

ARCHBISHOP It has had its advantages.

CONYNGHAM They have escaped my observation, I'm afraid.

ARCHBISHOP The Princess has not seen a great deal of her uncles. Her education has been – safeguarded.

CONYNGHAM (*extenuatingly*) Well, of course, I know – I know – I know.

ARCHBISHOP (*less extenuatingly*) Yes, my Lord, we *know*.

CONYNGHAM Had we not better sit down? We may have to wait. If that man's stone-throwing is not good – we may have to wait a long time. . . . So this is how history gets written!

ARCHBISHOP *This* won't get into history, my Lord.

CONYNGHAM No . . . Your Grace? – may I? . . .

(*He offers a flask-cup, after filling it.*)

ARCHBISHOP Ah, no. I thank you.

CONYNGHAM It's a chilly hour to be up. I never go about, late at night, or early – without *something*.

(*Drinks.*)

ARCHBISHOP For you, my Lord, very wise, I've no doubt. But I never go out at night, you see; at least, not late.

CONYNGHAM Ah! I often wish I didn't, when the night is over.

ARCHBISHOP That is – understandable.

CONYNGHAM (*missing the note of sympathy*) It's only human nature, your Grace.

ARCHBISHOP Yes, I suppose so. I don't know . . . My office . . . There is a good deal of human nature that I have to avoid.

CONYNGHAM Rather difficult to avoid at the Court of the Regency, wasn't it?

ARCHBISHOP Oh, of course, sometimes I had to – well – look the other way. Still, I attended so seldom; only when called on officially.

CONYNGHAM Your Grace has officiated on a similar painful though auspicious occasion, I believe?

ARCHBISHOP Yes. Yes. I announced his accession to His late Majesty King William. But he was only in the next room waiting.

CONYNGHAM Ah! How did he take it?

ARCHBISHOP With alacrity . . . 'Bless my soul! you don't say so!' were his first words. And then – 'Well, well, though I'm less of a figure-head, I shall make a better King than poor George.'

CONYNGHAM But he didn't, you know.

ARCHBISHOP No; a better character, but not a better King. That sometimes happens, I'm afraid.

c

CONYNGHAM Yes, kings often manage to do quite well without morals. Brain is more important.

ARCHBISHOP Not too much of that either, I should have thought. Don't those with brain give much more trouble to their ministers?

CONYNGHAM Oh, they manage to do that without any! His late Majesty was a conspicuous example of it. You wouldn't believe – no, you wouldn't believe the trouble we sometimes had with him. They say you can make a donkey go by tying a carrot in front of its nose. Well, he was like a donkey with a carrot tied to its tail.

ARCHBISHOP Really?

CONYNGHAM Just like that. Over the Reform Bill, you know, we almost had a Revolution – almost. Not *his* fault that we didn't.

ARCHBISHOP (*discreetly*) Was he just a little – like his Father, you know?

CONYNGHAM Mad, eh? No, not mad. It was the shape of his head, I think. It was pear-shaped, you know – just like a pear. 'The weakest fruit drops earliest to the ground,' says Shakespeare. Well, his head was weak fruit distinctly – amazing how it *hung on*: one can't exactly say 'lasted.'

(*The* FOOTMAN *re-enters.*)

Well? What have you done?

FOOTMAN I've called the maid, my Lord. Would your Lordship like more light?

34

CONYNGHAM Oh yes; a little more light would, I suppose, be better. (*Then to the* ARCHBISHOP) For so auspicious an occasion.

FOOTMAN The windows, my Lord?

CONYNGHAM No, no, not the windows, I think. *The blinds — the blinds* must stay down at any rate.

(*The* FOOTMAN *lights more candles.*)

ARCHBISHOP (*confidentially*) Very sad, very sad, you know! Good old King George — such a large family — so many sons, and not one of them what he should be.

(*Exit* FOOTMAN.)

CONYNGHAM (*grimly*) And she — the daughter of one of them.

ARCHBISHOP Ah, but women are different — so different, you know. Let's hope! Let's hope!

CONYNGHAM Well, we must get her married; and then — married to the right man — the difference won't so much matter — her Cousin, Prince George of Cambridge, would be very suitable — same age, and can talk English now, so I'm told, like a native.

ARCHBISHOP Over that you will have difficulty with the Duchess.

CONYNGHAM Oh, yes; the Duchess is going to be difficult whatever's proposed. She will regard this as her own succession almost.

ARCHBISHOP (*wisely*) It almost will be.

CONYNGHAM That is what we must *prevent*.

ARCHBISHOP The Duchess has privately planned a marriage more to her own liking, I'm told.

CONYNGHAM Eh? Who?

ARCHBISHOP She has two nephews – through her brother the Duke of Saxe-Coburg – Prince Ernest, and Prince Albert.

CONYNGHAM But that won't do! Tainted blood! Tainted blood!

ARCHBISHOP Indeed!

CONYNGHAM (*disgustedly*) Ye-es: bleeding skins – haemophilia. It's in the family. Cousins. No; it won't *do*.

ARCHBISHOP But Prince George is her cousin, also.

CONYNGHAM Ah, but it's not on that side. It's on the mother's – the Coburgs. And, you know, it comes through the women. The males have it: the women don't; but they pass it on. Do you know her brother, the Duke, once nearly bled to death?

ARCHBISHOP Dear me! Is that so?

CONYNGHAM Marrying her daughter to *his* son would be fatal! You know, it's all very well, in one way, for Royalty to make itself a class all by itself. But it's a German notion: 'tisn't English. And when it leads to so much inbreeding, it gets dangerous. English kings have married commoners in the past; they'd better do it again – or into the peerage. Do you know – if the Duke of Wellington had been – well, twenty years younger, I'd have married her to him.

ARCHBISHOP You don't mean it!

CONYNGHAM I do. 'Twould have been very popular; and a foreign marriage won't be. (*He looks at his watch.*) Tut, tut! That girl's a very long time coming!

ARCHBISHOP (*correctively*) The Queen?

CONYNGHAM (*plausibly covering his mistake*) No, no; I mean the maid. I'm wondering whether she has called her . . . It's a pity you know, a pity! I don't know what to think of it!

ARCHBISHOP 'It' meaning what?

CONYNGHAM A female on the throne; a King would have been so much better.

ARCHBISHOP I don't know, my Lord. Heirs male of the last generation have not been a conspicuous success.[1]

CONYNGHAM No English King has been a conspicuous success since Edward I.

ARCHBISHOP Yet the monarchy has – gone on.

(*Enter* MAID-SERVANT.)

CONYNGHAM Yes; but it's gone off.

MAID I beg pardon, my Lord.

CONYNGHAM Yes? Well?

MAID Her Royal Highness, my Lord. I went in, but Her Royal Highness was asleep.

CONYNGHAM Well, you must wake Her Royal Highness up then.

[1] This remark, having been ruled out of one of my plays by the Lord Chamberlain, now goes into another.

MAID Such a beautiful sleep, my Lord: I didn't like to.

CONYNGHAM Even the most beautiful sleep must give way to affairs of State. You know who I am?

MAID Yes, my Lord.

CONYNGHAM You know His Grace?

MAID Yes, my Lord.

CONYNGHAM Then go at once: wake Her Royal Highness, and tell her that we are here, waiting – for an audience.

> (*Awestruck and submissive, the* MAID *goes. A clock strikes.*)

Six o'clock. There is to be a Council at ten.

ARCHBISHOP Where? Here?

CONYNGHAM At St. James's, I imagine. No, perhaps it will have to be here. She mustn't appear in public yet. 'Twouldn't be quite decent. People might cheer.

> (*Enter the* DUCHESS OF KENT: *she is robed rather than dressed; but her heavy negligée has a certain dignity about it. She enters, a conscious 'Presence.' They rise and bow.*)

DUCHESS Your Grace, my Lord Conyngham, you have news for us?

CONYNGHAM For Her Royal Highness the Princess, we have news, Madam.

DUCHESS Ah! The King then – ?

CONYNGHAM Is dead.

DUCHESS Then my daughter is now – ?

38

CONYNGHAM Queen.

DUCHESS It has come, then – at last! And I – I am the Queen Mother!

CONYNGHAM No, Madam: your Royal Highness is not the Queen Mother.

DUCHESS (*affronted*) Not?

CONYNGHAM Your Royal Highness is the Queen's Mother; that is the distinction. Only had your Royal Highness been Queen in the first place, would that other title now follow.

DUCHESS Then, if it is not mine by your laws, she shall give it me.

CONYNGHAM That, Madam, I fear, will be impossible.

DUCHESS Ah! I will go myself and speak to her at once. That shall settle it!

CONYNGHAM Madam, we are here to see Her Majesty the Queen on urgent business; and we must not be delayed. Your presence at the interview, Madam, will not be required, unless Her Majesty sends for you.

DUCHESS Ah! This is not to be borne!

ARCHBISHOP (*conciliatory*) Madam, this is a very historic occasion. We are here officially only. Etiquette and immemorial tradition prescribe certain rules which have to be observed. Your Royal Highness would not wish to break them.

CONYNGHAM (*at centre*) Your Grace, she's coming!

ARCHBISHOP Then, Madam, for a moment – for a moment only!

> (*He opens a side-door and bows the* DUCHESS *through it. She goes compelled, but reluctant. The shadow of* QUEEN VICTORIA *is projected upon the wall of the lobby as she descends. The* ARCHBISHOP *and the* LORD CHAMBERLAIN *kneel and kiss her hand. The side-door opens again; the* DUCHESS *thrusts in her head; she watches spell-bound.*)

CONYNGHAM Your Majesty, it is our painful duty –

DUCHESS (*not waiting for the sentence to finish*) Ah! my daughter, she is Queen – Queen!

> (*The curtain slowly descends; after a few seconds it rises again.* VICTORIA *stands alone at the foot of the stairs. Away to the right, ceremoniously backing from the Presence, the* ARCHBISHOP *and the* LORD CHAMBERLAIN *make their last bow and go. Into this solemn scene no* FOOTMAN *intrudes; they let themselves out. At the sound of the shutting door, the side-door opens fully: the* DUCHESS *enters, and advances rapturously to claim her daughter's homage.*)

VICTORIA (*still a little mazed at the wonder of it all*) Mama!

DUCHESS (*embracing her*) My child! My child! Oh, my child!

VICTORIA They came to tell me that I am Queen.

DUCHESS Yes: you are Queen at last!

VICTORIA But really Queen – *now*: before I have been crowned?

DUCHESS Yes: now, at once! The King is dead: you are Queen!

VICTORIA Then my reign has already begun? I can do – as I like?

DUCHESS Yes; as you like! Do not mind what anyone says. If you want to do it – do it!

VICTORIA Oh! . . . Then . . . Mama. There is something I would like.

DUCHESS Ah, yes! Say it! say it! It shall be done.

VICTORIA How strange that it should have all come – so suddenly!

DUCHESS Yes, so suddenly – after we have waited so long. But now, my love – do not stay here to catch cold. Come back to your own Mother's bed!

VICTORIA No, Mama dear. As I may now do as I like, I wish in future to have a bed, and a room of my own!

DUCHESS (*stupent*) *Of your own?*

VICTORIA Yes – please, Mama.

DUCHESS Oh! so you have been waiting – for *that*!

VICTORIA I should be glad, if you don't mind – now that I am my own mistress. Yes, I would rather be alone.

(*She does not wait to hear more.*)

DUCHESS Mind! . . . Glad! . . . Alone! . . . O God! What is going to become of me?

41

(She stands and watches, while VICTORIA, *mistress henceforth of her own destiny, turns and goes quietly upstairs again, having imposed, even now, her wish to be alone for a while.)*

Scene III

The QUEEN *is still in mourning but she does not mourn. Animated and happy, she sits listening to what, in earlier youth, she was never allowed to hear — the conversation of a gentleman of breeding, worldly, witty, and to a certain extent wise. This she thoroughly enjoys. And* LORD MELBOURNE, *her Prime Minister, enjoys talking to her. She is not clever; she cannot say clever things; but the mingled strain of artlessness and self-possession, of dignity and simplicity, which he finds in his Royal Mistress's character — a character which he is artfully moulding, not so much to his own ends as his own convenience — attracts and delights him. They are now on such intimate terms that the* QUEEN, *when he comes for an audience, does not keep him long standing. They are seated now; and as an indication of their pleasant relations, the* QUEEN *is going on with her wool-work.*

VICTORIA How do you begin the day, Lord Melbourne?

MELBOURNE Begin it, Ma'am?

VICTORIA Yes. What do you do first — you, who have

42

so many things to do in the day? I find it difficult to know myself where to begin.

MELBOURNE Well, starting at the very beginning, Ma'am, I breakfast – if I may be allowed to say so – in bed.

VICTORIA Oh! I should never have thought of that!

MELBOURNE Try it, Ma'am; try it! It makes an invaluable break between sleeping and waking. Sleeping is one thing: it takes time. Waking is another: it takes more time. Working is another: and takes more time than all the others put together.

VICTORIA And after breakfast, what then?

MELBOURNE Well, let me think!... First, I rise, Ma'am. Over that I need not go into details.

VICTORIA No?

MELBOURNE Or – would you like me to, Ma'am?

VICTORIA (*a little disappointed*) No, oh, no. You rise?

MELBOURNE I rise from my bed. Then I ride in the Park; when I come home I write. So I begin with the three R's.

VICTORIA But 'write' begins with a W.

MELBOURNE I am corrected, Ma'am. 'Write' *does* begin with a W. Your Majesty is right, as usual.

VICTORIA (*laughing*) Oh! you are funny, Lord Melbourne.

MELBOURNE Funny?

43

VICTORIA So witty, I mean. You always say something amusing. Yes; please go on!

MELBOURNE That, Ma'am, is all the beginning of my day. When that is done, the day is half over.

VICTORIA And when do you say your prayers, Lord Melbourne?

MELBOURNE My prayers? Oh, I say them whenever I have time for them.

VICTORIA (*a little shocked*) But – Lord Melbourne!

MELBOURNE As often, and as long as possible.

VICTORIA That seems to me a little irregular.

MELBOURNE Did your Majesty never hear the story of the holy monk who had a Vision vouchsafed to him: a Vision of – well, of a very high character? And just as the Vision appeared, the chapel-bell began ringing. Duty – discipline – required the monk to leave the seraphic Vision and go into chapel with the rest: a function which, in these circumstances, was so like praying to the Vision behind its back, that it seemed almost foolish. It was a hard thing to do; but the monk did it. In great anguish of spirit, he left the Vision to itself, and went and did his duty. The service seemed intolerably long; he was dying to get back to his Vision. At last he was able to do so. The Vision was still there; and as he fell down before it in renewed adoration, the Vision made this remark: 'If you had not answered that bell, I should not have stayed' – or words to that effect. Ma'am, my position as Prime Minister is very similar to that of the pious monk. I am constantly having to leave the vision to answer the *bell*.

VICTORIA I thought, Lord Melbourne, that visions were rather superstitious things.

MELBOURNE They are, Ma'am. In these days they are! Do your best to avoid them. They savour too much of Roman Catholicism. And so, Ma'am, with your Majesty's permission, let me, for the moment, leave visions and come down to facts, and the affairs of State. There are certain things which will have soon to be decided; and one or two in which delay – delay of preparation at all events – is inadvisable.

VICTORIA Oh, yes; there are many, I'm sure.

MELBOURNE There is one especially, which your Majesty graciously deigned to mention the other day. You then said, Ma'am – with a courage which I thought remarkable in one so young – 'Some day we must marry' ... Has your Majesty given that matter any further thought?

VICTORIA Oh, yes, Lord Melbourne, I have thought of it a great deal.

MELBOURNE Is your Majesty prepared yet to take me into your Majesty's gracious confidence?

VICTORIA You mean?

MELBOURNE As to the possible recipient of so overwhelming an honour.

VICTORIA Oh, I have not thought of any person – in particular. I mean, I have made no decision.

MELBOURNE I am relieved to hear it, Ma'am. Then your Majesty has still an open mind?

VICTORIA An open mind? Oh, *of course*, I shall make my own choice, Lord Melbourne.

MELBOURNE Why, of course, Ma'am. I would not suggest otherwise, for a moment.

VICTORIA But there are certain things as to which I am quite resolved.

MELBOURNE As for instance?

VICTORIA My marriage, Lord Melbourne, must be a marriage of affection.

MELBOURNE That, I am sure, Ma'am, can be arranged without difficulty.

VICTORIA Someone, I mean, whose character I can respect: one whom I can love and look up to.

MELBOURNE Look up to?

VICTORIA Yes, Lord Melbourne, it may sound strange to you; but I must have as my husband one whom I can eventually look up to – when I have trained him for the position he will have to occupy.

MELBOURNE Oh, quite so, quite so. I trust that such a person will be found. And as your Majesty has owned to an open mind on the subject, I have here with me a list of – of possibles.

VICTORIA Oh, Lord Melbourne, how interesting! . . . How many?

MELBOURNE Well, at present, Ma'am, only five. But more are coming.

VICTORIA Coming?

46

MELBOURNE That is, I am making inquiries about them.

VICTORIA What kind of inquiries?

MELBOURNE All kinds of inquiries, Ma'am: my bounden duty. I would not wish to present your Majesty with one to whom there could be any possible objection.

VICTORIA And you have already found *five*! Lord Melbourne, how clever of you!

MELBOURNE 'Possibles,' I said. The inquiry is still going on; I am making it now. After inquiry of your Majesty, possibly there will be only one left.

VICTORIA I would like to see your list, Lord Melbourne.

MELBOURNE If your Majesty will pardon me a moment. When I have fully explained the considerations which guided me in my selection, I will submit my list for your Majesty's judgment, and (as I hope) approval.

VICTORIA I cannot approve all five!

MELBOURNE Just as a preliminary, Ma'am, why not? From five in the running select your favourite – the winner.

VICTORIA Perhaps I shall not choose one for a long time. But go on; I am quite interested and excited.

MELBOURNE The conditions, Ma'am, for a suitable consort to your Majesty's throne are necessarily special and particular – I might even say, peculiar. He must, of course, be of Royal blood; on the other hand, he must not be the direct or likely heir of any foreign king or reigning prince.

VICTORIA But why not, Lord Melbourne?

MELBOURNE Political complication might arise, Ma'am. The crown of Hanover has passed from your Majesty to another, because of the law which limits the succession to males only: a circumstance which I regard as fortunate. We want no more crowns of Hanover; the country is better without them. To proceed, then: he must be a Prince of some Royal House, not too petty, not too important. We must avoid entangling alliances. He must also be of the Protestant faith.

VICTORIA Oh, yes, *I couldn't* marry a Papist.

MELBOURNE You could not, Ma'am. The Act of Settlement forbids it. He must be sufficiently young to be a suitable life-partner to your Majesty. He must know, or be capable of learning the English language; capable also of adapting himself to English customs, habits, and prejudices. The last is the most difficult of all, since the English have a prejudice against foreigners.

VICTORIA But, Lord Melbourne, that makes it impossible!

MELBOURNE No, Ma'am. It only rather restricts the choice. Someone must be found who, once naturalised, is able to share the prejudice. I've known it done. Your Majesty's cousin, Prince George of Cambridge, for instance, is rapidly acquiring a thoroughly British outlook. In another five years or so he will have learned to dislike foreigners as much as we do.

VICTORIA But do *you* dislike foreigners, Lord Melbourne?

48

MELBOURNE No, Ma'am, no: of course not! But sometimes, for political reasons, one has to pretend to.

VICTORIA Well, and what more?

MELBOURNE It would also be well, Ma'am, if he had some means of his own; though they need not be large. Parliament will provide whatever addition is necessary. He must have presence suited to his station; also a certain amount of brain, but not too much. He must not expect to interfere in politics.

VICTORIA Indeed, no! I should never allow it.

MELBOURNE Finally he must have health, and a sound constitution; he must – that is to say – come of good stock. And that, Ma'am, has been our main difficulty. Good stock, in the Royal Families of Europe, is rare.

VICTORIA Please explain, for I don't quite understand. 'Good stock' – I thought that meant cattle.

MELBOURNE It does, Ma'am, in certain connections. But it also means – what comes from father to son. You find it referred to in the Second Commandment where we are told that the sins of the fathers are visited on the children: also their virtues. In certain Royal lines the sins and the virtues have been mixed; and one has to be careful that they shall not be more mixed. For that reason the marriage of Royal cousins is generally inadvisable.

VICTORIA Oh.

MELBOURNE Generally, I say. In the case of a certain branch of your Majesty's family connections it is unfortunately true in a rather special degree. For that reason,

D

in the list I am about to submit, I have not included — though it was suggested to me — two of your Majesty's cousins, who might otherwise have been desirable candidates — their Royal Highnesses Prince Ernest and Prince Albert of Saxe-Coburg Gotha.

VICTORIA But they both looked quite strong and healthy when I last saw them two years ago.

MELBOURNE Apparently, Ma'am. But appearances are sometimes deceptive. It is, of course, a delicate — even a painful subject. But, acting under medical advice, and with a due sense of my responsibility, I have not included either of those young Princes in the list which I have now the honour to present to your Majesty.

(He rises, and puts the list into her hand: hurriedly she glances down the names.)

VICTORIA Oh, but do I know any of them?

MELBOURNE Your Majesty knows one of them very well.

VICTORIA Oh — I didn't see. But Prince George is my cousin too.

MELBOURNE By another branch, your Majesty. There is not there the same objection.

VICTORIA Oh, but I couldn't marry my Cousin George! He is so — so —

MELBOURNE Nobody wishes to decide your Majesty's choice. There are others.

VICTORIA But, as I say, I don't know any of them.

MELBOURNE That, Ma'am, can easily be remedied. You ask them to your Court in turn, saying nothing. And you let them go away again – saying nothing; or you *do* say something; and then – either they stay, or they come again.

VICTORIA But it is for me to decide, is it not?

MELBOURNE It is for your Majesty to decide. Your Majesty need not marry at all.

VICTORIA Oh, but I must marry. Mama always said so.

MELBOURNE So I have been told. But in so important a matter, even devoted filial affection should not be allowed to influence your *choice*. I have merely indicated, Ma'am, that were any attempt to be made to influence your choice in a certain direction, that choice – for reasons already given, I should have to oppose.

VICTORIA Lord Melbourne, I should not allow any opposition in a matter of that kind. It would not influence me for a moment.

MELBOURNE No?

VICTORIA Indeed, rather the other way.

MELBOURNE I see. I understand, Ma'am. I sympathise. I shall say no more. I will only commend the matter to your Majesty's good sense – and conscience.

VICTORIA Oh, how kind you always are to me, Lord Melbourne! What a lot you are teaching me!

MELBOURNE What a lot you are teaching *me*. I have served under older sovereigns – under two. But I have never served under one who listened to advice so wisely or so well.

VICTORIA (*rising*) Good-bye, Lord Melbourne. Will you keep the list, or shall I?

MELBOURNE By your leave, Ma'am; let what I have said be either remembered or forgotten. (*He tears the list and throws it into the fire-place.*) The choice must be your own.

VICTORIA Yes; but you haven't yet shown me — any portraits.

MELBOURNE Portraits, Ma'am? Why portraits?

VICTORIA I can't decide about anyone — till I know what they are like. It wouldn't be fair to them — or to me.

MELBOURNE But your Majesty can send for them, and see.

VICTORIA Oh, no. I'm not going to send for any, if I don't like the look of them.

MELBOURNE Portraits are sometimes deceptive, Ma'am.

VICTORIA Yes; I saw a portrait of my Cousin George of Cambridge the other day: quite handsome he looked.

MELBOURNE I can get their portraits, Ma'am, if you wish. But Court Painters, like Prime Ministers, know their duty; and they only do what is expected of them. If they can't do that, they have to go.

VICTORIA (*going toward a table, on which stands a framed portrait*) Here is a portrait that was sent to Mama, the other day — of my Cousin, Prince Albert.

52

MELBOURNE (*who has followed to the table*) Oh! Ah! Yes. H'm.

VICTORIA Surely *he must* have grown very handsome! It would not be possible for a Court Painter to imagine anyone like that.

MELBOURNE You never know, Ma'am: you never know. Imagination sometimes goes a long way. Well, the list having gone, am I now to make a collection of portraits for your Majesty?

VICTORIA Oh, no, Lord Melbourne. I wasn't speaking seriously when I said that.

MELBOURNE No more was I, Ma'am. But I do ask your Majesty to *think* seriously. The future welfare of this country is now in this little hand.

(*He stoops and kisses it.*)

VICTORIA Indeed, Lord Melbourne, I pay great attention to everything that you say. And I shall continue to take your advice, whenever I find it – possible. Good-bye.

(LORD MELBOURNE *bows himself out. She goes and takes up the portrait and kisses it.*)

Albert . . . Albert . . . Albert . . . will you marry me?

SCENE IV

LORD MELBOURNE, *the Prime Minister, sits in his writing-room at Downing Street. With him is* MR. TUDOR, *British Minister at the Court of Saxe-Coburg*

Gotha, now on home leave. The Prime Minister lolls indolently at ease; so far the official report has not much interested him. MR. TUDOR sits upright in his chair, precise and respectful. He is much the younger man; but already he has been taken into the confidence of persons of importance; and is not without a certain sense of his own.

MELBOURNE Yes? Well? What also have you to report?

TUDOR The Court of Saxe-Coburg is a little anxious, my Lord, because nothing has been said lately about the possible arrangement – of a marriage.

MELBOURNE (*his interest awakened*) Ah?

TUDOR The Court is anxious, my Lord, because the Princes are now of marriageable age; and it doesn't want to let good chances slip.

MELBOURNE Are any other brides in the market, then?

TUDOR For His Royal Highness Prince Ernest there is the prospect of a very eligible offer. But a rumour of this other possibility has got about; and they won't make the offer if it is going to be refused.

MELBOURNE So they want the coast cleared for Prince Ernest, eh? What about Prince Albert?

TUDOR I have reason to believe that they would prefer it should be Prince Ernest.

MELBOURNE And I have reason – very grave reason – to prefer that it should be neither. Anyway, let Prince

54

Ernest go. Tell 'em to give him away to anybody as quick as they like. That'll be one off my mind, at any rate.

TUDOR Your Lordship does not now favour the proposal, then?

MELBOURNE I never did. It was the Duchess with her damned interference. She seems to think this country was invented entirely for the benefit of her own family. 'Twas she made the match, as far as it could be made.

TUDOR Is Her Majesty greatly under the influence of Her Royal Highness the Duchess, my Lord?

MELBOURNE Not now; no, not now. But she is greatly under the influence of her own feelings. And it so happens that – before I could be there to prevent – the thing was done. She has seen both of them. Oh, yes; she'd have liked Prince Ernest well enough, if Prince Albert hadn't been there also.

TUDOR At Saxe-Coburg they do not wish it to be Prince Albert, my Lord.

MELBOURNE What they don't wish is not going to count. I'm afraid, I'm very much afraid she will go her own way in this matter. She's in love with him. She kisses his portrait, I'm told. And it's very serious – very serious indeed. Cousins of that stock marrying may be *fatal*.

TUDOR If your Lordship wishes to prevent the marriage with Prince Albert, it can be done quite easily.

MELBOURNE I've been trying all I know how. And it's God damn difficult. She shut me down – as if I were nobody. I've tried more than once.

TUDOR It need not be difficult, my Lord. You have merely to state certain facts, and – the match will be off.

MELBOURNE Well, now you do interest me exceedingly! Already morganatically married to some German wench, eh?

TUDOR Oh, no, no. Nothing of that sort. The Prince has a blameless character. The same cannot be said about his late mother, the Grand-Duchess.

MELBOURNE No, so I . . . His parents separated over something, I believe.

TUDOR They separated when the Prince was five years old. She went to live in Paris; he never saw her again. The *cause* of the separation was of *more* than five years' standing, my Lord. (*This is said with meaning.*)

MELBOURNE (*rising, with sharp interest*) Heh? . . . You don't say so!

TUDOR After five years the parties forgot to be prudent: the thing got about.

MELBOURNE (*sitting down*) Who was – the *other* party?

TUDOR One of the Court Chamberlains: a very charming and accomplished person; but a commoner, and of Jewish extraction.

MELBOURNE (*pondering deeply*) Dear me! Dear me! . . . *Healthy?*

TUDOR Oh, quite. . . . You have only to tell Her Majesty that her cousin, Prince Albert, is not quite so much her cousin as she imagines, and I apprehend that you will have no further difficulty.

MELBOURNE (*following his own line of thought*) The *Mother* was healthy, was she not?

TUDOR Well, she produced two fine boys. But *Prince Albert is the finer*.

MELBOURNE Then only Prince Ernest is really related?

TUDOR That is so.

MELBOURNE And the Duke can't be the father of Prince Albert?

TUDOR Unfortunately, no.

MELBOURNE You are sure?

TUDOR I have confidentially been shown documents which put the matter beyond dispute. In the deed of separation the facts were fully admitted.

MELBOURNE Why were you shown them?

TUDOR I imagine, my Lord, because at Saxe-Coburg there is a wish that Prince Ernest should be Her Majesty's choice — not Prince Albert.

MELBOURNE (*rising, in a tone of deep satisfaction*) Ah! . . . Mr. Tudor, I am enormously obliged to you — *enormously* obliged to you. Your information is a godsend! And — if my term of office holds for a while, as I think it will, I can promise you promotion. The next suitable vacancy will be yours. Understand: you have done your country a great service.

TUDOR (*who has risen at the same time as his chief*) My Lord, I thank you.

MELBOURNE I thank *you*! Good-bye.

(MR. TUDOR *bows over his hand with deep respect,
and goes.* MELBOURNE *rings, and walks about
excitedly. A* SECRETARY *enters.*)

MELBOURNE Has Lord Conyngham waited?

SECRETARY Yes, my Lord.

MELBOURNE Then ask his Lordship to be good enough
to come in.

(*The* SECRETARY *goes.* MELBOURNE *sits down,
writes, gets up again, rubs his hands. He is as
happy as a schoolboy. Enter* LORD CON-
YNGHAM.)

MELBOURNE Conyngham, we've done the trick! We
are going to marry her to Prince Albert.

CONYNGHAM (*aghast*) Good Heavens! You don't say
so! . . . But —

MELBOURNE (*going up to him, and speaking with an
intensity of significance which at last has its effect*) It's all
right! . . . It's all right! . . . *It's all right!*

CONYNGHAM But, my dear Mel, what has made it —
'all right,' as you say?

MELBOURNE *Human nature.*

(*And at last the* LORD CHAMBERLAIN *comprehends.*)

CONYNGHAM Well! It seems almost like — Divine
Intervention.

MELBOURNE It was, Conyngham, it was! It isn't only
marriages that are made in Heaven. Liaisons are made
there too. Thank God!

58

Scene V

The DUCHESS *sits in the same apartment in Kensington Palace as in Scene I. But now new splendours have been added to it. Before her stands* LADY CHARLOTTE — *one of her Maids of Honour.*

DUCHESS So; she said that you were to go? What did you say?

LADY CHARLOTTE Madam, I only said that my appointment was to the Household of your Royal Highness.

DUCHESS Ah! You said that! Good! And she — what?

LADY CHARLOTTE She said that, when your Royal Highness had a separate household of your own, there would be no further objection.

DUCHESS 'Separate!' . . . 'Separate!' She has not yet said that to *me*; but she has meant it. It has been coming, from the first day: her own bed, her own room — now it is her own house. Presently it will be her own country that I am not to share! (*Enter* VICTORIA.) So! You are sending me away!

VICTORIA Mama!

DUCHESS You are turning your own Mother out of doors.

VICTORIA Lady Charlotte, go, please!

DUCHESS Why is she to go? She is mine: she is not yours.

(But without further word, the look of direct authority has been sufficient. LADY CHARLOTTE *disappears.)*

VICTORIA Mama, I wish you would not speak to me like that before — servants.

DUCHESS Servants? Lady Charlotte is my friend, one of the few I have left.

VICTORIA You pay her for her service.

DUCHESS *You* are paid for *your service* too — the country pays you. Does that give it the right to dismiss you at a week's notice?

VICTORIA Mama dear, don't be foolish.

DUCHESS Oh, what has happened to you? You are no longer the same!

VICTORIA How can you expect me to be? I belong now to myself. I find that a great change.

DUCHESS And who made you be — yourself? What had you done *for yourself*, till you got rid of me?

VICTORIA Very little, almost nothing. For eighteen years I was not even allowed to go downstairs without somebody to hold my hand. But I did it sometimes, when no one was looking.

DUCHESS Behind my back?

VICTORIA Yes. I would look out from the room. If there was a servant-in-waiting, I would send them on an errand. Then — when I was quite sure that no one could see — I would run down — down and up again, as fast as I

60

could go. That was about my only chance of doing anything, *for* myself, by myself.

DUCHESS Then you were deceitful.

VICTORIA Had you asked me, I should have told you. I have never told you an untruth, Mama; and I am not going to begin now.

DUCHESS Then now tell me the truth – quick! Do you any longer love me?

VICTORIA Of course I love you, Mama.

DUCHESS Though you take from me everything that is mine.

VICTORIA On the contrary, dear Mama. I am going to give you something more than you have ever had before. Often now I have to leave you alone.

DUCHESS Yes.

VICTORIA But not so much alone, in one sense, as you would like to be. You and Lehzen do not get on well together.

DUCHESS We do *not*. Why do you keep her? She was only your governess. Send Lehzen away.

VICTORIA No, Mama.

DUCHESS 'No, Mama!' 'No, Mama!' It is always 'No, Mama,' now to everything I ask you.

VICTORIA When you said you did not wish to go to Windsor last week, did I make you go?

DUCHESS No, but you only put it off. I do not like

Windsor. It reminds me of your Uncle too much. It was there that he insulted me before everybody.

VICTORIA   You need not go to Windsor now, unless you like, Mama.

DUCHESS   Need not go? If you go to Windsor, I must.

VICTORIA   No, Mama. It is not necessary now. Should I need you, I can send for you.

DUCHESS   But — you are not going to Windsor without *me*! It would be in all the papers.

VICTORIA   I want you to have a change, Mama. It will do you good; and I am sure that, when you have tried it, you will like it. I have given directions that in future you are to have your own suite of apartments at Buckingham Palace, with a separate service of your own. Next week, when I go to Windsor, it will be ready for you.

DUCHESS   I do not like Buckingham Palace. I am not going there . . . I say that I am not going there . . . Do you hear me? I am not going to Buckingham Palace, I am going to Windsor.

VICTORIA   You are mistaken, Mama dear. You are not going to Windsor, for I do not invite you. I will do so later. When Ernest and Albert pay their promised visit, it will, of course, be necessary that you should be there.

DUCHESS   Then I will not come!

VICTORIA   I don't think we need discuss the matter any further: the date is not yet fixed. And now, Mama, about Lady Charlotte; for I see that she has been speaking to

62

you. When you have a Household of your own, I shall not interfere. If you wish then to have Lady Charlotte as one of your Maids of Honour, she can come back to you again. Here, for reasons with which I need not trouble you, I do not wish her to remain.

DUCHESS So!

VICTORIA And if you stayed with me, Mama, there would have to be *other* changes.

DUCHESS What do you mean?

VICTORIA I would rather not say. I hope that, in the short time you are still with me, it may not be necessary.

DUCHESS Oh, why is there always now this — this opposition? This *battle*? It never happened before.

VICTORIA Often, Mama. But *then* you always got your way. If it is painful to you now when I decide things for myself, think how painful it used to be to me, when I was never allowed to.

DUCHESS You throw my training of you back into my teeth, eh? You would have liked better to be with those wicked Uncles of yours, with their wine, and their women, and all!

VICTORIA Mama, don't forget yourself.

DUCHESS Forget myself!

(*Enter* LEHZEN.)

VICTORIA Ah, Lehzen dear, is it already time for me to come?

63

DUCHESS Let that woman go! I have not said yet all that I want to say!

VICTORIA Good-bye, Mama.

DUCHESS Victoria, I am your Mother, and I command you to stay!

> (*But* VICTORIA *and* LEHZEN *have gone. The* DUCHESS *sits down to weep.*)

DUCHESS To think that this should have happened to me, of all people!

> (*Enter* SIR JOHN CONROY.)

CONROY Dear Lady, what is the matter?

DUCHESS My daughter is the matter.

CONROY I met Her Majesty just now, with the Baroness.

DUCHESS Did she say nothing?

CONROY Nothing.

DUCHESS Did she look at you?

CONROY Yes: she looked at me.

DUCHESS You bowed: did she return it?

CONROY Hardly.

DUCHESS You are going to be the next — if she can manage it. But I shall not let it be. No; she shall not send you away — my friend.

CONROY What has happened?

DUCHESS To-day she takes from me one of my friends. Lady Charlotte is to go. Yesterday I was not to dress myself as I liked.

64

CONROY Not dress?

DUCHESS No! . . . I had my dressmaker there. I was going to leave off some of all this stuff and nonsense which I am wearing for a man that hated and insulted me. She said the dates for change of mourning were all in the Court circular, and must be obeyed. And when I asked her if I was expected to consult the Court circular, she said yes, as long as I stayed at the Court; which was almost like telling me to go away. And when I asked was she still in deep mourning for having become Queen, she said, 'Don't talk nonsense, Mama dear!' That – to *me*! Whenever she has anything unkind to say to me now, she puts 'Mama dear' at the end of it. I always made her say it when I punished her for anything. Now she says it to punish *me*.

CONROY Why do you still stay with her? Aren't you free now to go where you like?

DUCHESS Oh, how can I go away from my own life? She was everything to me. And now to her I am nothing! There is only one thing now left me to work and hope for. When that is done I shall just go away to my own country – and die.

CONROY What is that, dear Lady?

DUCHESS Just to see her married to Albert or Ernest. I planned it from the day she was born. But I'm beginning to be afraid even that won't happen now. Oh, what a miserable woman I am! And I thought I was going to be so happy!

CONROY Dear Lady, don't make me feel that I am useless.

E

DUCHESS You? What can you do? She won't take advice from *anybody* now, except that wicked Melbourne. And he hates me. It is all *his* doing. She could not have changed to me like that, unless someone had come between.

CONROY (*embracing her*) My dear Lady, and mistress!

DUCHESS Oh, my friend! I am so utterly alone!

CONROY Alone? No: not while you have *me*.

DUCHESS Oh, yes, I have *you*. But if she knew – or even guessed – it would be all over. She has no pity for anyone. Human nature means nothing to her – nothing!

CONROY (*renewing his embrace*) While to us it means so much! Everything.

(*Enter* VICTORIA. *They break apart.*)

DUCHESS I thought you were going out with Lehzen.

VICTORIA (*coldly*) Have I returned sooner than you expected, Mama?

DUCHESS Oh, it does not matter.

VICTORIA No? (SIR JOHN, *meanwhile, is making for the door.*) Do not go, Sir John. I have something I wish to say. I am making certain alterations in the arrangements of my Household. You have been told of them, perhaps, and were taking your leave of Her Royal Highness when I came in. As I do not wish that there should be any delay in the matter, let it be so. You will see the Comptroller before you go. I have given directions that a solatium shall be paid to you in recognition of your past services. You will leave to-day.

66

DUCHESS You are sending away my friend?

VICTORIA I did not know he was your friend, Mama.

DUCHESS You shall not! This is unheard-of. It is monstrous!

VICTORIA No, Mama; not monstrous, only wise.

DUCHESS I will not allow it! I will not allow it! If he goes, you kill me.

VICTORIA Mama! Sir John Conroy, will you retire?

DUCHESS Do not! Do not move! (*She rushes to the central door and stands barring it.*) He shall not go!

> (*Undiverted, the* QUEEN *points quietly to another door, which has no tragic figure standing before it.*)

VICTORIA *That* door, Sir John.

> (*Such perfect common-sense commands the situation. Without hesitation he goes.*)

DUCHESS (*coming away from the door, her defence of it now useless*) Oh, you – you – you, that was once my little daughter! That I taught to be so good!

VICTORIA You, my Mother, that I was taught to think so good.

DUCHESS What do you mean? What do you say?

VICTORIA Nothing – that needs repeating.

DUCHESS Oh, you have no heart in you! You are harder than a stone wall. If you can no longer respect me – have you no pity?

VICTORIA Pity?

67

DUCHESS Yes, what is my life without you? What has my life been for? Why did your Father and I marry? For you to be born. He did not love me: I did not love him. It was for *you*. No, *he* did not do it for *you*. *He* wanted a son. When you came, he was disappointed. But I – I was not. He died, and you were everything to me. And ever since, I have been alone – *except for you*. Then you became Queen, and you are mine no longer; all at once you are your own, and I am *nothing*! And I am to live without love, and to have no friend? You see a little love offered to me – nothing wrong – just friendship, kindness, and you take it away from me, you drive him away. But he shall come back to me – he shall come back!

VICTORIA Mama dear, when you have a Household of your own, you will have in it whoever you like. I said so before; if it will be any comfort to you, I say it again. I have had to send Sir John Conroy away because here, it seems to me, he does not know his place. What his place is likely to be in the future, when the matter is in your own hands, I see only too clearly.

DUCHESS Victoria, you forget yourself!

VICTORIA No, Mama; the forgetfulness is yours.

DUCHESS I forget *nothing*!

VICTORIA Then, please to remember, Mama dear, that you are now my subject.

DUCHESS (*hardly believing her ears*) Your *what*?

VICTORIA If you wish me to repeat the word, I will. All my duty of obedience to you is over. It is now rather the other way.

68

DUCHESS Oh! Oh! This is too much! – This to be the end of all my care of you! Have I become the mother of a revolting daughter?

VICTORIA Of a reigning Queen, Mama.

(She seats herself at the writing-table.)

I am going to write some letters now, Mama; and I would prefer to be alone. I am going to invite Ernest and Albert to come and stay at Windsor early next month; and I shall want you to be there, so please make no other engagements.

DUCHESS *(to herself)* Ernest! Albert! Ah, then I am not quite dead yet. So you are writing to them? Very well. My love to both of them – especially to Albert.

(She goes out. A FOOTMAN *enters.)*

FOOTMAN If it please your Majesty, Lord Melbourne asks if he may see your Majesty.

VICTORIA Ask Lord Melbourne to come in.

(She continues writing, till MELBOURNE *enters. Then goes to meet him.)*

Dear Lord Melbourne, I am so pleased to see you.

MELBOURNE That is kind of you, Ma'am: but your Majesty is always kind. I also am pleased – more pleased even than usual – to see your Majesty; for I have come to inform your Majesty of a happy circumstance.

VICTORIA Yes?

MELBOURNE In a matter where I feared we were going to differ somewhat seriously, we now see eye to eye.

VICTORIA About what, Lord Melbourne?

MELBOURNE As regards your Majesty's proposed marriage –

VICTORIA But, Lord Melbourne, I have not proposed marriage to anyone.

MELBOURNE Matrimonial intentions, then, let me say – (*Very respectfully he takes up the portrait of* PRINCE ALBERT *and looks at it.*) I now withdraw all opposition. In fact I cordially agree. I think your Majesty's choice is excellent. In your hands the future welfare of the country is safe.

VICTORIA Oh, that is very kind of you, Lord Melbourne; and I am glad to hear it. But I feel bound to tell you that, even had you *not* agreed, it would have made no difference at all.

MELBOURNE No, Ma'am. The facts being what they are, it *would* have made no difference at all. Not the least!

VICTORIA I wanted you to know that, Lord Melbourne.

MELBOURNE (*bowing acknowledgment*) And the Prince comes – when, Ma'am?

VICTORIA Next month, I hope.

MELBOURNE Next month, let us all hope! And what, Ma'am, does Her Royal Highness the Duchess think about it?

VICTORIA Mama will be pleased, I'm sure.

> (*She takes the portrait from his hand and kisses it. But – she does not know – the facts!*)

MELBOURNE 'Mama' ought to be very pleased, indeed – with such a daughter!

70

The Wicked Uncles

Characters

PRINCESS AUGUSTA	*A future Queen*
THE DUCHESS OF BENDIGO	*Her Mother*
THE DUCHESS OF CUMBER	*Her Aunt*
THOMAS, DUKE OF CUMBER	
DUKE ERNEST	
DUKE OCTAVIUS	*Her Uncles*
DUKE FREDERICK	
PRINCE GEORGE AUGUSTUS OF FLAMBOROUGH	*Her Cousin*
MISS ANGUS	*A Lady-in-Waiting*
MR. TURNBULL	*The Duke's Chaplain*
JOSEPH BUNNY	*The Duke's Valet*
A MAID-SERVANT	
A FOOTMAN	

The Wicked Uncles

Scene I

*A Sitting-room in the Town House of H.R.H. The Duke
of Cumber.*

*Three of the Royal Brothers have met for consultation.
In hobnobbing proximity, there they sit — as obviously
wicked as any group of elderly men can, by their exteriors,
make obvious the inward dissoluteness of careers now
drawing to a close.* THOMAS, *Duke of Cumber, is the
leading spirit; but it is* DUKE OCTAVIUS *who speaks
first; and if deeds could come out of words, the* DUCHESS
OF BENDIGO *would die a cat's death.*

DUKE OCTAVIUS The old Cat!

DUKE THOMAS Leave the old Cat out! Her Kitten's
got to marry some day.

DUKE ERNEST But they'll have to get old King Jimmy's
consent to it. If she could have done it legally without,
the Cat would have got her married already.

DUKE THOMAS She's only got to wait a bit. Poor
Jimmy's not going to last long.

DUKE OCTAVIUS Seen him lately?

DUKE THOMAS Went down to Hanzor to see him yesterday – about this very matter.

DUKE OCTAVIUS H'm! Well?

DUKE THOMAS Oh, he's game for it all right. Anything to spite the old Cat would suit him – in reason. But the poor old boy says to me: 'Tom,' he says, 'I must have some conscience and morals to finish with; so near my end as I am now!'

DUKE ERNEST What did you say?

DUKE THOMAS I said, 'Don't worry about damned notions of that sort for another ten years. You won't want 'em till then.' But I couldn't say it as if I believed it. He gave me a kind of a look. 'Ah, Brother,' he says, and starts crying.

DUKE ERNEST Well, well! He was tough enough till a year ago, except for his gout. Then he seemed all to crumple.

DUKE OCTAVIUS You told him we'd fixed on George Augustus, as the other party?

DUKE THOMAS Why, yes; so'd he. But he says she won't have him; and can't make her, he says. 'A hard little bag of tin-tacks,' that's what he called her.

DUKE ERNEST The Kitten?

DUKE THOMAS The Kitten. He's seen more of her than we have, you know.

DUKE ERNEST Now that the Cat won't let us be on speaking terms!

DUKE OCTAVIUS And why won't George Augustus do for her? Isn't he good enough? In the family — first cousin — same age — healthy — steady, so far — and good-looking enough, considering.

DUKE ERNEST Hasn't much chin, though.

DUKE OCTAVIUS Good chins don't run in our family; he's none to boast of. His chin's as good as hers; and his morals too.

DUKE ERNEST Oh, indeed! Where did you get that?

DUKE OCTAVIUS Up to yesterday, at any rate, still a virgin; so his parson-tutor told me.

DUKE THOMAS (*properly shocked*) God! You don't say so!

DUKE OCTAVIUS *I* don't. *He* does. Locks him into his room every night, and never lets him loose in the day.

DUKE ERNEST Huh! There's always a window, though.

DUKE THOMAS Window? Yes. That's how I got my damned limp when I was sixteen. They did much the same to me. 'Twas no good.

DUKE OCTAVIUS Ah, George Augustus isn't a climber. Hasn't the legs for it.

DUKE THOMAS A man's legs follow what's over 'em — when he's after the women. . . . Still (*meditatively*), that was yesterday. I put *you* on, to get him away from that parson of his.

DUKE OCTAVIUS So I shall to-morrow. Augustus is coming to stay with me; and I told his tutor I shouldn't

77

have room for *him*. So the boy'll get his first taste of freedom.

DUKE ERNEST And before he can turn round in it, we are going to marry him. Poor devil! 'Tisn't fair.

DUKE THOMAS Oh, he can have his freedom afterwards. He'll be the King Consort then – when Jimmy's gone; and Jimmy won't last another year.

DUKE OCTAVIUS Shall any of us?

DUKE THOMAS Damn it, man! Don't croak! Anyway, this is a little game worth playing, isn't it? Spite the old Cat!

DUKE ERNEST What does Brother Fred say? Does he know? Will he be with us?

DUKE THOMAS He knows. I told him yesterday. He hadn't stopped chuckling over it when I came away. Yes he'll be with us whenever we fix it – if his gout lets him. And it's practically fixed now.

DUKE ERNEST And Jimmy agrees to the marriage – when?

DUKE THOMAS There was no time-limit. To-morrow, if we can manage it. I put it to him as a thing to be done – and done soon. 'A marriage in the family,' I said, 'one we can all approve of – will brighten things up for you.' He agreed right enough. 'Do it if you can,' he said, 'but the damned Duchess won't let you. Once she gets wind of it, she'll raise hell, and the country too. How are you going to do it behind her back?'

DUKE OCTAVIUS Yes; how are you?

78

DUKE THOMAS Well, I was for telling him. But he took fright and stopped me – didn't want to hear. So we left it at that. *How* don't matter. I've got his consent.

DUKE ERNEST Tom, you've got some plan up your sleeve?

DUKE THOMAS (*contemptuously*) Yes. Shouldn't be hoping to get one out of *you*, if I hadn't.

DUKE ERNEST What is it?

DUKE THOMAS You shall hear. (*Gets up and rings the bell.*) It's what you've come for. (*Helps himself to drink.*) (*Enter* BUNNY, *the* DUKE'S *confidential man-servant.*) Bunny, tell His Royal Highness, and *His* Royal Highness, what you were telling me last night.

BUNNY If you please, your Royal Highness;[1] which means – telling what?

DUKE THOMAS The result of your inquiry into the domestic habits of Her Royal Highness the Duchess of Bendigo, and of her daughter, the Princess, and of the household generally.

BUNNY Oh, very regular, your Royal Highness.

DUKE THOMAS Very regular – yes?

BUNNY Always the same every day, your Royal Highness. Same hours for getting up and going to bed. Breakfast at eight, prayers at nine. Then comes three hours' lessons for Her Royal Highness the Princess; then –

DUKE THOMAS You can leave out the rest of the day. What about bed? When do they go?

[1] Mr Bunny pronounces it 'rileness.'

BUNNY Her Royal Highness, the Princess, goes at ten o'clock, your Royal Highness; and Her Royal Highness, the Duchess, goes at eleven.

DUKE THOMAS Yes, and what did you find out about Saturday?

BUNNY Every Saturday night, your Royal Highness, the Princess takes a bath.

DUKE THOMAS In her own room?

BUNNY No, your Royal Highness, in another room where a bath is put ready for Her Royal Highness.

DUKE THOMAS And that always at ten o'clock on Saturday night?

BUNNY Yes, your Royal Highness.

DUKE THOMAS And the same when she goes anywhere to stay?

BUNNY If it can so be arranged, your Royal Highness. Sometimes there isn't a bath to be had.

DUKE THOMAS Have *we* got a bath?

BUNNY Oh, yes. Your Royal Highness has two; but only one in general use, so to speak, your Royal Highness.

DUKE THOMAS H'm! New-fangled notion having baths. It's a dirty habit. Sweating's the way to keep clean. That'll do, Bunny, you can go.

(BUNNY *retires.*)

DUKE ERNEST Well?

DUKE THOMAS Well, that's my plan. Order of the

bath. Goes into it a Venus, comes out of it a married woman.

DUKE OCTAVIUS I don't see where the bath comes in. He can't get into it with her.

DUKE THOMAS Next door to it. I can get 'em into a bathroom, here in my own house.

DUKE ERNEST The old Cat won't let her come, if she knows you're here.

DUKE THOMAS I shall be away – till the time comes. Then we shall all be here, ready. Nobody'll know. The house is large enough. I've a private door of my own. . . . You begin to smell it?

DUKE ERNEST (*almost shocked*) You don't mean to say your going to make George Augustus . . .?

DUKE THOMAS Rape her? No. I'm going to make George Augustus marry her. And I'm going to make *her* marry George Augustus. We shall *all* make her. She's only a little chit of a thing. She can't hold out against the whole Family, and the King's consent. Call it his dying wish; true enough. He'd like it to happen before he dies; and he is dying. Besides, it's my belief she hates her mother –

DUKE OCTAVIUS (*interjecting*) That shows sense, anyway.

DUKE THOMAS – and I'll be glad to get quit of her. And the shorter the cut, the better she'll like it.

DUKE ERNEST It'll be no short cut if the Cat gets wind of it first.

DUKE THOMAS She won't. Shan't give her time. All done while they think she's having her bath. That's the

F

plan. When Mamma comes up to bed at eleven, she finds Pussy married.

DUKE ERNEST And how'll you get her into the house?

DUKE THOMAS The invitation has gone already, and I'm going to be away; at least, I've said so. The old mother Cat and my Duchess are friends after a fashion – though me she won't speak to. The Duchess has got some family jewels she's been meaning to give Augusta – some day. So all I had to say was – 'Have her to stay with you next Saturday and over Sunday.' She comes; she takes her bath – we see to it she has her bath – she goes to it a maid, and she comes from it married. That's my plan. Can you think of a better?

DUKE OCTAVIUS It's damned risky.

DUKE THOMAS Take the risk, and it's damned easy.

DUKE ERNEST Does George Augustus know?

DUKE THOMAS Not yet. Of course he'll have to know, I suppose. We'll have to tell him on the night.

DUKE OCTAVIUS That means you are afraid to tell him before. What if he says no?

DUKE THOMAS He won't. Tell a lad of spirit, who's been cooped up as he's been – and never allowed to look at a woman, alone – that he'll have one to spend the night with, first time in his life. D'you think he'll say 'no' to that? And is sharing the crown nothing? He'll have dined; he'll be feeling like a gentleman; he'll have all of us to back him. He sees her; we provide the parson, and the thing's done. What d'you think of it?

82

DUKE OCTAVIUS Who's the parson?

DUKE THOMAS My own chaplain; at least I keep him. He don't say prayers for *me*. I shall tell him to do his duty without asking questions. And marrying people isn't a sin; so *his* conscience won't need to trouble him.

DUKE ERNEST Well, Thomas, if you want to know what I think of it – I think you're either the damnedest rascal that was ever born with royal blood in him, or you are a man sent from God. I dunno which. But whichever it is, I'm with you, heart and soul. Ha! ha! ha!

(*An uncontrollable fit of laughter seizes him.*)

DUKE OCTAVIUS What are you laughing for? This seems to me a bit serious. Suppose it doesn't come off?

DUKE THOMAS But it will.

DUKE ERNEST I'm laughing at the old Cat, Ocky. She'll be here in the house, under the same roof, while the thing's going on. Sends Kitten to have her bath! In an hour goes up herself, expecting to find Kitten in bed. Kitten won't be there. Kitten'll be having her Tom.

DUKE THOMAS Her Augustus, you mean. Tom's my name.

DUKE ERNEST And Tom's your nature! Ho! Ho! Ho! (*He laughs uproariously, and helps himself to drink.*) Here, Tom, a toast for all of you, 'The Old Cat.'

(*The three Wicked Uncles help themselves, and raise their glasses.*)

All. 'The Old Cat. Damn her!'

CURTAIN

A few days later the DUCHESS OF CUMBER *is entertaining her expected guests. State has been waived for the occasion, for the* DUCHESS *is a good deal of an invalid; and most of her days are spent in the small boudoir, where the chairs are so much more comfortable, and where four ladies are now sitting. The* DUCHESS *has with her* AMELIA, DUCHESS OF BENDIGO, *the* PRINCESS AUGUSTA, *and* MISS ANGUS, *the* DUCHESS'S *own lady-in-waiting.* MISS ANGUS *sits respectfully removed from the rest, nearer to the* PRINCESS AUGUSTA *than to the two elder ladies, whose conversation she is not supposed to listen to until she is invited. The* PRINCESS AUGUSTA, *who also sits somewhat removed, is doing her wool-work, for it is one of Mama's rules that when her mind is idle her hands must not be. And she also is supposed not to listen unless invited to. So with a presumably unoccupied mind she works; and when she drops a skein of wool,* MISS ANGUS *picks it up for her. Except when service is thus required of her,* MISS ANGUS *sits rigidly idle; it is her duty; occupation for her would be disrespectful.*

DUCHESS CHARLOTTE I hope you don't mind our being alone, Amelia?

DUCHESS AMELIA Not at all, Duchess dear. When you so kindly invited us, you promised that we should be alone.

DUCHESS CHARLOTTE Oh, yes. The Duke told me he

had engagements all this week, so I could say so quite safely. He generally has, you know. So much to do in the public eye. And you too, my dear, having to take Augusta about so constantly, so that she may be seen and known by everybody.

DUCHESS AMELIA (*with a warning look*) I take Augusta about so that she may *see and learn*, Duchess. It is for her education only that I do so.

DUCHESS CHARLOTTE But you find the people . . .?

DUCHESS AMELIA Oh, yes, always very pleased to see us, of course; very loyal and respectful.

DUCHESS CHARLOTTE Ah . . . yes.

DUCHESS AMELIA But I have not trained Augusta to have any great opinion of herself – or of her position, at present – *not yet*. (*This is said with meaning.*)

DUCHESS CHARLOTTE Oh . . . indeed? Then . . .

DUCHESS AMELIA For the present, I think it *better*.

DUCHESS CHARLOTTE (*with lowered voice*) Then she doesn't know?

DUCHESS AMELIA That she will be Queen some day. Not yet.

DUCHESS CHARLOTTE Dear me! What a surprise it will be for her when you do tell her, my dear.

DUCHESS AMELIA I am training her, my hope is, so that *nothing* shall ever surprise her. It is so important that she should be self-possessed. That above everything. It is, indeed, part of her lessons. Every day we do an hour of *savoir-faire*.

DUCHESS CHARLOTTE How interesting! How do you do it?

DUCHESS AMELIA Augusta!

AUGUSTA Yes, Mama.

DUCHESS AMELIA Leave the room!

AUGUSTA Yes, Mama.

(*She rises, curtsies, and goes towards the door.*)

DUCHESS AMELIA That will do, Augusta. Go back to your seat. I was only showing your Aunt Charlotte how well I have trained you — *in obedience*.

AUGUSTA (*curtsying*) Yes, Mama.

DUCHESS AMELIA You see?

DUCHESS CHARLOTTE Well, now, that is wonderful! At her age that she can stand it.

DUCHESS AMELIA At her age! Why, Duchess, she is only a child; she is only seventeen!

DUCHESS CHARLOTTE I was married at seventeen, Amelia; and had had my first . . .

DUCHESS AMELIA (*a little shocked*) Oh, Duchess dear!

DUCHESS CHARLOTTE But it was too small; it died. . . . After that I had five more, but they all died. I never could understand why. The Duke said it was my fault, not his. But there!

DUCHESS AMELIA Where is the Duke now?

DUCHESS CHARLOTTE Oh, I don't know, my dear. I never try to know. When he is at home, he always stays in bed until twelve o'clock. His breakfast goes up to him.

Then he sends word to me whether he will be dining or not. Sometimes he does, but not often. If he does, we dine at four. But after six he always has some engagement. And *I* never go out, you know; not now.

DUCHESS AMELIA No?

DUCHESS CHARLOTTE My entertaining days are over.

DUCHESS AMELIA But your Grace is still quite entertaining.

DUCHESS CHARLOTTE Very kind of you to say so, my dear. No, I never go out now. Ah, but that reminds me of something. I knew there was something. My memory is beginning to fail me; so I have to ask Miss Angus to remember for me instead. (*Beckoning.*) Miss Angus, what was that of which you were to remind me, when the Princess was here?

MISS ANGUS (*advancing*) There was a box your Highness showed me.

DUCHESS CHARLOTTE A box? Ah, yes. You know which it is? Can you get it?

MISS ANGUS Oh, yes certainly, your Highness.

DUCHESS CHARLOTTE Then do.

(*Exit* MISS ANGUS.)

Augusta, my dear, do you know that I was married fifty-two years ago?

AUGUSTA Why, Aunt Charlotte, that must have been just when Mama was *born*.

DUCHESS AMELIA Not quite, my dear. Nor has my birth anything to do with it.

87

DUCHESS CHARLOTTE When I was married – I have just been telling your Mama – I was younger than you, my dear. And my Aunt, the Princess Wilhelmina of Schleswig, gave me a present of some pearls – beautiful pearls they were then. I was married in them, and I have had them ever since. They were thought quite fine in those days; but since then the fashion seems to be for larger ones. So now they live in a box, and I have sent Miss Angus to fetch them; for I am going to give them to you, my dear.

AUGUSTA Oh, Aunt Charlotte, how kind of you! Pearls!

(MISS ANGUS *returns with the box, which she takes to the* DUCHESS OF CUMBER.)

DUCHESS AMELIA Very kind of your Aunt, I'm sure. And just what I would wish for you. Pearls are so much more suitable for a young girl than stones which are of more value.

DUCHESS CHARLOTTE (*To* MISS ANGUS.) Ah, yes. Thank you! There, my dear; open the box, and look at them.

AUGUSTA Oh, how beautiful! Oh, thank you, Aunt Charlotte! Thank you so much! May I kiss you?

DUCHESS CHARLOTTE Yes, kiss me, my dear. And listen: I want you to wear them on the day that you marry. Will you?

AUGUSTA Why, yes! Nothing could be nicer.

DUCHESS CHARLOTTE And I hope they will bring you as good a husband as they brought me.

88

(At this the DUCHESS OF BENDIGO'S *face is a picture.)*

AUGUSTA *(impulsively)* Oh, they will, I am sure!

DUCHESS AMELIA *(acidly)* That is not very nicely said, Augusta.

DUCHESS CHARLOTTE Oh, but I know quite well what she means. Yes, my dear, you will be happily married some day. And I hope they won't all die like mine did.

DUCHESS AMELIA Duchess dear!

AUGUSTA Did you have more than one husband, Aunt Charlotte?

DUCHESS CHARLOTTE No. I wasn't talking of husbands my dear. No.

DUCHESS AMELIA Put them back in the box, Augusta, for the present. You can look at them again when you go upstairs. And when I come I will lock them up safely.

DUCHESS CHARLOTTE I don't know whether you know, Amelia, that pearls ought always to be worn; that, if they are not frequently worn, they lose their lustre.

DUCHESS AMELIA Yes, I believe so.

DUCHESS CHARLOTTE Well, of course, I used to wear them a good deal; but of late years I have had no occasion to wear them; and recently I noticed that they were beginning to go off. Well, what was I to do? I didn't like to let my maid or anyone else wear them. It didn't seem somehow that anyone else ought to wear the pearls my Aunt Wilhelmina had given me for myself. So I used to make Fido wear them, because Fido didn't matter.

89

Fido always slept in my room at the foot of my bed – such a dear doggie he was. And every night he used to come and wag his tail, and have his pearls put on. Till, at last . . . No, he wouldn't go to sleep until he had them. He was quite human about it. And then, last year, poor Fido died; and nobody has worn them since – nobody. So I thought it really was time I gave them to somebody else, before they went bad.

DUCHESS AMELIA (*not very well pleased*) Very kind, and thoughtful, and timely, I'm sure.

AUGUSTA (*sentimentally*) Poor Fido. I shall always think of him now when I wear them.

DUCHESS AMELIA (*dryly*) A touching memory!

DUCHESS CHARLOTTE Oh yes, he was a very good little dog.

> (*With soft, silvery tone, the clock on the mantelpiece strikes ten.*)

DUCHESS AMELIA Augusta, my dear, it's ten o'clock. Your bath. Put up your needlework. So kind of you, dear Duchess, to let her have a bath. I hope it wasn't too inconvenient.

DUCHESS CHARLOTTE Oh no; it has all been arranged. We haven't what is *called* a bathroom; but there is a room where a bath can be put when one is wanted. I don't take baths myself; my health doesn't allow it. But young people, I suppose, it doesn't hurt – not if they are accustomed to it.

DUCHESS AMELIA Augusta always has one on Saturday night. I have taught her to look upon it as a fitting preparation for the Sunday.

DUCHESS CHARLOTTE A very pretty idea, I'm sure. Yes, good-night, my dear. It isn't in your own room, but the maid will come and show you the way. And you needn't be afraid to come out of your room, for nobody else will be about. Good night, and I hope that you will sleep well.

AUGUSTA Good night, Aunt Charlotte. And thank you so much for these beautiful pearls. When I go upstairs I shall put them on, just to see.

DUCHESS AMELIA You will not wear them in your bath, Augusta.

AUGUSTA (*who had been meaning to*) Why not, Mama?

DUCHESS CHARLOTTE That would not be decent.

AUGUSTA (*at a loss to know why*) Oh?

DUCHESS AMELIA Go, my love. I shall not be long. Mind that you are in bed by the time that I come up.

AUGUSTA Yes, Mama.

DUCHESS CHARLOTTE You think you can find the way, my dear, upstairs – to your room?

AUGUSTA Oh yes, I'm sure I can!

MISS ANGUS (*who goes to open the door for her*) A maid is waiting outside to attend your Highness. She will show your Highness the way.

(*Curtsies her out.*)

AUGUSTA Thank you.

(*She goes, taking the box of pearls with her.*)

DUCHESS AMELIA From what I have seen of it, this seems to be a very large house.

DUCHESS CHARLOTTE Yes, it always has seemed large, having no family. Once I lost my way in it. It was in the dark and going back to my room the candle blew out. And I went down the wrong passage and into the wrong room, and got into the wrong bed. But there! — I never found out till the morning. And when I woke up there was somebody else, *not* my husband, lying asleep beside me — so fast asleep that, luckily for me, he did not wake — so that I got safely back to my own room without anyone knowing. But just fancy, Amelia, suppose Thomas had missed me! It would have been very awkward.

DUCHESS AMELIA Very awkward indeed!

DUCHESS CHARLOTTE Oh, Amelia, I have just remembered who it was. It was his brother, Ted — your husband!

DUCHESS AMELIA I'm not at all surprised.

DUCHESS CHARLOTTE Well, it never happened again. And I had almost forgotten it. Curious that your coming should have reminded me.

DUCHESS AMELIA (*dryly*) The association, I suppose.

DUCHESS CHARLOTTE With your husband? Do you know, I think it was almost the last time I saw him — lying there asleep.

DUCHESS AMELIA Under such circumstances, a very suitable memory for you to have. Mine is more lively.

DUCHESS CHARLOTTE (*with a sigh*) Ah, well! We have

92

all lived at some time of our lives! And now, Amelia, wouldn't you like a little music before we go to bed?

DUCHESS AMELIA Delighted, I'm sure.

DUCHESS CHARLOTTE Miss Angus, will you sing to us, please?

MISS ANGUS With pleasure, your Highness. What would your Highness like me to sing?

DUCHESS CHARLOTTE Do you like Scotch songs, Amelia? You see, Miss Angus is Scotch; so that is what she sings best.

DUCHESS AMELIA I'm afraid I do not understand the Scotch language.

DUCHESS CHARLOTTE Oh, but she sings them in English, don't you, Miss Angus? Let the Duchess hear you sing the 'Allan Water' song. That is such a sweet song, so sad. I always cry directly it begins, because I know what is coming.

DUCHESS AMELIA I don't like songs that make me cry.

DUCHESS CHARLOTTE Don't you? Oh, I do. I do. Crying is such a comfort, when you've nothing better to do. It's so soothing to the nerves. Yes, Miss Angus, begin.

(MISS ANGUS *sings the first verse of 'Allan Water.'
The* DUCHESS OF CUMBER *begins weeping. The
curtain falls; the second verse follows.*)

*The room, all swept and garnished, has a sense of waiting
for something: the devils in occupation do not yet number
seven. Certain arrangements indicate preparation for a
ceremony. Across a spacious entrance at back hang
crimson curtains. In front of them a prie-dieu has been
placed, with kneeling-cushions for two. To the left is a
door shut off from the room by a high folding-screen;
opposite is a fireplace with an architectural super-
structure of bust and urns. A console stands in each
corner. To right and left of the fireplace are a chair
and a settee. A chair stands to either side of the central
entrance; down-stage from the screened door is another
chair. Into this sparse furnishing comes an importation —
a low wheeled chair bearing the ponderous form of*
DUKE FREDERICK. *He sits with swathed legs sup-
ported by a foot-rest.* MR. BUNNY *charioteers him into
place on the up-stage side of the door-screen. Having
done so, he brings a spirit-stand and glasses within
convenient reach of the wheeled chair, and re-closes the
crimson curtains. The Duke's brother is already there
to receive him.*

DUKE THOMAS Welcome, Royal Brother! Glad to see
you! So you've managed it, eh?

DUKE FREDERICK Thought I wasn't going to. Haven't
been out for a month; and doctor says I oughtn't to be out
now. But I don't go by what doctors say — never did! . . .
(*He helps himself to a drink.*) Well?

94

DUKE THOMAS Oh, all smooth so far . . . Bunny, come and tell me when everything's ready.

BUNNY Yes, your Royal Highness.

DUKE THOMAS Which way do they come?

BUNNY Through *this* door, your Royal Highness. I put the screen, so as to make it more home-like for her Royal Highness.

DUKE THOMAS (*inspecting*) Oh yes, I see . . . yes, all right.

> (*Thus dismissed,* MR. BUNNY *departs. Meanwhile through the curtains the two other Uncles,* ERNEST *and* OCTAVIUS, *have entered. They have all very obviously dined, to say the least of it.*)

DUKE FREDERICK Hullo, Ernie!

DUKE ERNEST Hullo, Fred.

DUKE FREDERICK Hullo, Ocky. Where's your pup?

DUKE ERNEST We've got him safe in there. He's just making sure of himself; sitting down for a bit.

DUKE FREDERICK God damn my soul, Tom! You've made this place look like a church.

DUKE THOMAS So it ought! Bathroom, as you come in: church, as you turn the corner. But it does look more like a church than a bathroom, I must say.

DUKE FREDERICK Don't know what a bathroom's like; never seen one.

DUKE OCTAVIUS Tom, it's pretty near time, isn't it?

95

DUKE THOMAS Not far off.

DUKE OCTAVIUS How are you going to get her to come here?

DUKE THOMAS Oh, Bunny's managing it. He's got one of the maids who'll do anything for him. Judging from her appearance, she's done it already. The man knows his job; I leave it to him.

DUKE FREDERICK Got your parson?

DUKE THOMAS Book and all. Isn't he there, Ocky?

DUKE OCTAVIUS Yes, having a hard sweat over it, too. I've been screwing up his courage for him. It took a lot.

DUKE THOMAS Fetch him in.

DUKE OCTAVIUS Damn it all! He's your man, not mine. Fetch him yourself.

DUKE THOMAS (*raising his voice*) Mr. Turnbull!

> (*There is a pause. Stridently, a clock in the corridor without strikes ten. The curtains open.* MR. TURNBULL, *the Chaplain, in black gown and bands, steadies himself into view; but makes no attempt to advance.*)

TURNBULL Yes, your Royal Highness? Did your Royal Highness call me?

DUKE THOMAS I did. Come in! Oh, you've got yourself ready, I see. Right! What are you trembling about, man?

TURNBULL (*moving unsteadily towards the prie-dieu, the better to support himself*) I'm not sure, your Royal Highness, whether I shall be doing right.

96

DUKE THOMAS You'll only be doing as I tell you. Aren't I your master?

TURNBULL Yes, your Royal Highness; but I've got into trouble for doing *that* before.

DUKE THOMAS Well, weren't you paid for your trouble?

TURNBULL Oh, I'm not complaining, your Highness.

DUKE THOMAS Aren't you? I thought you were. What sort of trouble are you expecting this time?

TURNBULL Your Royal Highness will pardon me. There have been marriages in the Royal Family before, that *have* caused trouble.

DUKE THOMAS Yes, but this won't. Now you listen to me, Turnbull. The King knows of this one.

TURNBULL (*not quite comfortably*) So your Royal Highness has informed me.

DUKE THOMAS D'you doubt me?

TURNBULL No, your Royal Highness.

DUKE THOMAS Very well; then *he's* not going to make any trouble about it.

TURNBULL No, your Highness. But His Grace, the Archbishop, may.

DUKE THOMAS Let him!

TURNBULL For me — that might be serious.

DUKE THOMAS Look here, Turnbull; if the Archbishop hears of it, and makes trouble — serious trouble — I'll give you a thousand pounds. Can't say more than that, can I?

TURNBULL That is not for me to say, your Highness.

G

I wouldn't presume to put a limit to your Highness's generosity.

DUKE THOMAS Turnbull, you are not as drunk as you look.

TURNBULL No, your Highness, I hope not. I only mean that a pension for life would make me feel safer.

DUKE THOMAS Very well, Turnbull; pension for life then. And don't drink yourself to death, and make it a bad bargain.

TURNBULL No, your Royal Highness; it's only on exceptional occasions like this that I . . . exceed the limits of my calling.

(*Music is heard. The strains of 'Allan Water' come filtering in from a distance.*)

DUKE ERNEST What's that music? Somebody singing?

DUKE THOMAS Miss Angus, probably; the Duchess's lady. Sounds like her squall.

(*Enter* BUNNY. *He stands waiting to catch* DUKE THOMAS'S *eye. Then says, in low, discreet tone.*)

BUNNY If you please, your Royal Highness, Her Royal Highness, the Princess, has gone up to her room.

DUKE THOMAS Very well. The maid has her instructions?

BUNNY Yes, your Royal Highness.

DUKE THOMAS Then, as soon as Her Royal Highness is ready, we shall be ready too.

(BUNNY *goes.*)

Now, Brothers all, prepare yourselves for the great event! This is going to make history, you know. Ernest, you be best man; go and bring in the bridegroom. Ocky, you stand by, and as soon as she comes in, lock the door.

(DUKE ERNEST *goes through the curtains.*)

DUKE OCTAVIUS Wish I didn't feel so damned nervous about it all. You know, Tom, you've done more things of this sort than I have.

DUKE THOMAS Never done anything like it in my life. This is the first virtuous act I've ever done, in my senses, that I can remember. You understand, Turnbull – this is a virtuous act we are doing. We are saving a woman's honour. She's not married, she ought to be married; you are going to marry her . . . You got that?

TURNBULL Yes, your Highness. That is what your Highness told me in the first place, when the matter was first opened.

DUKE THOMAS Tell you again, then. And mind you, though no name has been mentioned – better not – the woman's a lady.

TURNBULL Of course that makes it . . .

DUKE THOMAS Of rank and position. You may never have seen her before, but you'll see her, from now on, pretty often. Great place in society; you'll have helped. It'll be something for you to be proud of. With that and your pension – we may yet make a bishop of you. Who knows?

TURNBULL If I have your Royal Highness's word for it, that your Royal Highness will see me through.

99

DUKE THOMAS Well, you have. Then there's the other party – the man. Who *he* is you may have guessed, though you've never seen him before. Where *is* the man? Time he was here. Ernest! (*Raising his voice*) Why don't you bring your man in?

DUKE ERNEST (*appearing at curtain*) All right. All right. I *am* bringing him. He's coming – gradually.

> (*And through the curtains, very gradually, but not very steadily,* GEORGE AUGUSTUS *enters. He has a fair, weak face, deficient in chin. His hair, which he wears long, had been elaborately done for him in high waves.*)

DUKE FREDERICK See the conquering hero comes!
Sound the trumpets, beat the drums!

DUKE THOMAS Come in, my dear boy! Very glad to see you. All of us are very glad to see you. This is a great occasion. And you know what the occasion is, don't you?

> (GEORGE AUGUSTUS *stands with glazed eyes fixed; for he is very young, and his hardened old Uncles have made him far more drunk than they intended to. Now, in answer to his Uncle's questions, he grunts out a flabby affirmative.*)

GEORGE AUGUSTUS Yeh!

DUKE THOMAS You know that you've come here to be married, don't you?

GEORGE AUGUSTUS Yeh!

DUKE THOMAS And you want to be married?

100

GEORGE AUGUSTUS Yeh!

DUKE THOMAS And you know who you are going to marry, don't you?

GEORGE AUGUSTUS Yeh.

DUKE THOMAS And you are doing it of your own free will, aren't you?

GEORGE AUGUSTUS Yeh.

DUKE THOMAS Nobody making you . . . You want to marry her, because you ought to marry her, eh?

GEORGE AUGUSTUS Yeh.

DUKE THOMAS And you'd *like* to marry her?

GEORGE AUGUSTUS Yeh.

DUKE THOMAS And you *mean* to marry her?

GEORGE AUGUSTUS Yeh.

DUKE THOMAS There you are, parson. You asked whether it was a forced marriage you were expected to perform. I said no. Now you've heard the consent of one of the parties; and you shall have the consent of the other. That satisfy you?

TURNBULL Yes, your Royal Highness. It's irregular; but as your Royal H . . .

DUKE THOMAS Have a drink, Turnbull.

(He fills a glass.)

TURNBULL Oh, your Highness, less than that would be better!

DUKE THOMAS Be a man! Be a man! Can't have too much of a good thing. You haven't got to preach a sermon;

only to read a service. And you've got your book with you. As soon as we get the two of 'em together, and I give the word, you begin. By the by, who's got the ring? Anyone got the ring? Ernest, why the Hell, as best man, haven't you provided the ring?

DUKE ERNEST Because any ring'll do, so long as she can wear it. Here's one. Put it in your pocket, Boy, so's to have it ready. And remember you give it back to me when the job's done.

(MR. BUNNY *enters by screened door.*)

BUNNY If you please, your Royal Highness, Her Royal Highness will be here in a few moments.

DUKE THOMAS Right. (*Exit* BUNNY.) Now then, Royal Brothers, be ready, all of you. Here! Stand him straight! Sit him in that chair, then! She's coming. Ocky, the door! Parson, your place!

DUKE FREDERICK Squad, 'shun! Present . . . ar-r-rms!

DUKE THOMAS Ssh!

> (DUKE ERNEST *places the too-swaying Bridegroom upon an up-stage chair, where he sits retired from the main action which is now to take place. The Chaplain takes up his post at the prie-dieu, supporting himself against it, unobservant of what goes on around him, his eyes half-closed.* DUKE OCTAVIUS *stations himself near the screen, but out of sight from anyone entering.* DUKE THOMAS *moves heavily across towards the fireplace.* DUKE FREDERICK *helps himself to a drink. Within the screen*

102

the door opens, and a maid enters, ushering in the PRINCESS AUGUSTA.)

MAID If your Royal Highness will step this way.

(*She stands back to make way for the* PRINCESS *to pass, and whisks out again, closing the door. Slowly* AUGUSTA *moves round the screen. She wears a pink dressing-gown trimmed with swansdown; and on her neck are the pearls. As she sights the assembled Uncles, she halts, puzzled, but not alarmed.* OCTAVIUS, *not very adroitly, slips past her and locks the door.*)

AUGUSTA I beg your pardon. I was told this was the bathroom.

DUKE THOMAS It's all right, my dear. Come in! Come in!

AUGUSTA But I think there must be some mistake.

DUKE THOMAS Not at all. It's all been arranged.

DUKE ERNEST We've been expecting you.

AUGUSTA Oh?

DUKE THOMAS Don't you know who I am?

AUGUSTA I think you must be one of my uncles. Uncle Frederick, is it not?

DUKE THOMAS No, no. I'm your Uncle Thomas; and it's my house you're staying at. *This* is your Uncle Frederick.

AUGUSTA (*not moving from her place*) Oh! How do you do?

DUKE THOMAS And that's your Uncle Octavius.

AUGUSTA How do you do?

DUKE THOMAS And this is Uncle Ernest.

AUGUSTA How do you do?

DUKE ERNEST How do *you* do, Augusta.

DUKE THOMAS Yes, that's really more important. How *do* you do, my dear?

AUGUSTA I am quite well, thank you, Uncle Thomas; and very much obliged to you for letting me come here; to your house, I mean.

DUKE THOMAS Oh, don't mention it. Very pleased, very pleased indeed. Pray sit down!

AUGUSTA Oh, but surely you don't want me to remain here any longer, *as I am now*?

DUKE FREDERICK Oh yes, we do! We do! We do!

AUGUSTA I didn't expect . . . I wasn't prepared . . . not properly dressed, I mean.

DUKE ERNEST Very prettily dressed, my dear. Nothing could suit you better: *(then, sotto voce)* except to be undressed.

AUGUSTA But isn't this rather . . .?

DUKE THOMAS Unusual? Yes, my dear, not only rather, but very – extremely. Affairs of State, when urgent and important, have a way of being 'unusual.'

AUGUSTA But how can any affair of State concern *me*, just now, I mean? For I was on my way to bed.

104

DUKE FREDERICK All in good time, Augusta. You are going to bed; but you are not going yet.

DUKE ERNEST We've something very important to tell you first.

DUKE OCTAVIUS Yes. Most important.

AUGUSTA Indeed?

DUKE THOMAS Couldn't be more important. Listen, Augusta. This is the most important and solemn day in your life.

AUGUSTA But how is that possible? I don't understand. Do, please, explain.

DUKE THOMAS My dear Augusta, your Uncle, the King, is very ill.

AUGUSTA Yes, so I was told yesterday.

DUKE THOMAS Well. To-day he's no better; and never will be.

AUGUSTA I'm sorry.

DUKE THOMAS Of course. We are all sorry. Well, that's what brings us all here.

DUKE ERNEST Yes, Augusta. It's because of your poor Uncle, the King, that we are here now.

DUKE FREDERICK Trying to carry out his wishes — his dying wishes.

DUKE THOMAS You see, Augusta, when he goes there will be a change, a great change. Someone else will have to come to the throne. A new reign.

AUGUSTA Yes, of course.

DUKE THOMAS And that somebody will have to marry, if they are not married already. The country will expect it of 'em. So, as the marriage has got to be, the sooner the better.

AUGUSTA But, Uncle, why are you telling me this? What has it to do with *me*?

DUKE THOMAS That's just what I'm trying to explain. You are still very young, Augusta. But a great decision has had to be made for you. The King has made it. The Family's made it. So now you must make it too.

AUGUSTA Anything I can do that the King wishes, and that is right, Uncle, I shall be only too glad to do.

DUKE THOMAS Why, of course, you couldn't do otherwise. Well, then, my dear. That's what we are here for. The King can't be here himself. We are here in the King's name, so as to get the thing done — and so that nobody else shall come interfering to prevent it being done.

DUKE OCTAVIUS (*rising to the occasion*) Of course we didn't want to make it too sudden for you, Augusta; that's why we've explained: that's why your Uncle Thomas has explained — to make you understand.

AUGUSTA But at present you haven't explained anything.

DUKE THOMAS Haven't we? I thought we had. Fred, you have a try, then.

DUKE FREDERICK My dear, it's quite simple. Listen. The King's your Uncle; he's an old man; and he's got no children — none that count. And there's only you and your Cousin George Augustus left of the whole family who can

106

marry now, and have children – that can count. So there it is – quite simple. Couldn't be simpler.

DUKE THOMAS So you see, my dear. It is, as I said, an affair of State, urgent and important. And it can't wait. The King wishes it, knows all about it, has given his consent. So, as his loyal subjects and servants, we are only doing what he wants us to do; and *you* are only doing what he wants *you* to do.

AUGUSTA But what *am* I doing?

DUKE THOMAS You are being married, my dear. Didn't you know? Hadn't you guessed? Why you must have done, for I see you've put your pearls on. And very pretty they look. 'Twas my idea. I told your Aunt I thought it was about time you should have 'em, so as to be married in 'em. And married in 'em you shall be, this very night.

AUGUSTA Married? But who am I to marry, Uncle?

DUKE THOMAS Sly little puss, pretending you don't know! That's your modesty, I suppose. Just look round and see who's here that you'd like to marry – most.

AUGUSTA But I don't understand why I should marry *anyone* – now – immediately.

DUKE THOMAS Don't you, my dear? Then sit down, and I'll explain.

AUGUSTA Please, I don't think I'll sit down, Uncle, if you don't mind.

DUKE THOMAS Won't you, my dear? Just as you like. But you must allow me to, for I'm getting old; my legs are not what they used to be. So you want me to explain, eh, why the matter is so urgent and immediate?

107

AUGUSTA Please, Uncle.

DUKE THOMAS Well, it's because of the *law*. If you were to marry without the King's consent – not as *he* wished, but as your Mother wished, say – your marriage wouldn't be legal. So that's one of the things we've got to prevent.

AUGUSTA But indeed, Uncle, I should not allow Mama to decide for me on such a matter as that.

DUKE THOMAS Shouldn't you? Well, that's one to the good anyway. And the sooner you let your Mother know it the better. And as it's the law that you can't be married legally without the King's consent, the only thing for you to do is to have his consent.

AUGUSTA Of course, I should always ask his consent, when the time came for it.

DUKE THOMAS Well, my dear, as, for all we know, he mayn't outlive the night, if you're to marry with his consent, you've got to be pretty quick. I can't put it plainer than that.

AUGUSTA But, Uncle, suppose that were to happen, then . . .

DUKE THOMAS Then, it would have to be with someone else's consent. And that wouldn't be your Mother's – though, with him out of the way, she might think so. And so, my dear –

(*He pauses: not really having anything more to say.*)

AUGUSTA Well, Uncle; and so?

DUKE THOMAS 'Well, Uncle; and so?' – You hear that?

108

She's got her pretty little head screwed on the right way, hasn't she? Stands up to her old Uncle as if she were a man! . . . Well, as I say, there's the whole thing in a nutshell. So long as the King's alive, what he wishes, we *all* wish. You can only be married by the King's consent. We've got the King's consent; and nobody else's consent matters a damn.

AUGUSTA Matters a what?

DUKE THOMAS Your Mother. You see, my dear, you've been born with Royal Blood in you from top to toe. You're one of the Royal Family. And one of the first things members of the Royal Family have got to learn is that they mustn't think of themselves; especially not when it's a question of marrying. You've got to think of the Crown, and the Country, and the People – what they'll expect of you; what'll make you popular – make the Crown popular, make the Royal Family popular. What'll make Parliament vote you a decent income to marry on: which they won't if they don't like it. It's often a damned nuisance, but it's got to be done. It's the King's wish that settles it, not yours. We didn't one of us marry the woman we wanted to marry – not one. I was lucky, some of the others weren't. And *you're* lucky; you haven't got to marry a foreigner. Most of us had to. And the Country don't like 'em – prefers its own breed; and I don't blame it. You're lucky, I say, because the King's going to let you marry someone you know, someone you like. And that's what brings us here now. Your Mother would stop it if she could, because she and the King don't get on together – don't agree about anything. But she can't, so you can leave her out.

AUGUSTA You can't leave Mama out for long, Uncle. She is here now, you know.

DUKE THOMAS My dear Gussy, we know all about it. Of course she's here, or you wouldn't be. You've never been allowed to have a soul of your own, or a will of your own about anything, have you? You haven't been allowed to know your own Uncles. Never had a day or an hour to do in as you liked. Well, from now on, you can set yourself free – open your cage – live your own life, *be yourself*. Married, she can't touch you; married, you become of age, and belong all to yourself – and your husband. And he won't rule you with iron and sticking-plaster like she's done. Gentle as a lamb. You'll be able to do anything with him – twist him round your pretty little finger as you like.

(*He pauses.*)

AUGUSTA Yes, Uncle. Well?

DUKE THOMAS That's the position, Augusta. And now everything's explained, and everything's ready. Here's the parson; here are we, the witnesses; here are you, with your wedding pearls on. And here's your second wedding present, the man himself. George Augustus, stand up and show yourself! Time's come. Parson, get ready to start! Now, Augusta.

> (MR. TURNBULL, *prodded into semi-consciousness, opens his eyes and his book, and starts reading the marriage service; till, finding he's not being attended to, he trickles back into silence, more deeply, but more solemnly drunk than any of them.*)

TURNBULL Dearly beloved, we are gathered together here in the sight of God and in the face of this congregation, to join together this man and this woman in Holy Matrimony, which is an honourable estate instituted by God in the time of man's innocency, etc.

(*Meanwhile* AUGUSTA, *after a short pause, is speaking with perfect self-possession.*)

AUGUSTA I'm sure it was very kind of you, Uncle, and all of you, to take so much trouble.

DUKE THOMAS No, my dear; not kind. The thing had to be done, and that's all about it.

AUGUSTA I mean – to have explained to me, so carefully and fully, why you thought it would be good for me. And I'm sure that you have all meant well. But –

DUKE THOMAS There's no 'but' about it, my dear. You didn't come here to 'but.'

AUGUSTA But, Uncle, there *is*. And you must, please, listen to me. I must decide this for myself.

DUKE THOMAS No, no, no! We know what's for your good better than you do. Parson, find your place again, and go on. You listen to *him*, my dear.

TURNBULL (*opens at the wrong place*) Remember not, Lord, our iniquities, nor the iniquities of our forefathers, neither take thou vengeance for our sins, etc.

AUGUSTA (*meanwhile*) I don't think he is in a fit state to be listened to, Uncle.

DUKE THOMAS George Augustus, come along and show yourself. Stand up to her; be a man!

AUGUSTA No, Uncle; it is not in the least necessary that he should do so. We are not attracted – either of us. I must wish you all good night. Uncle Octavius, you have the key. Unlock the door, please!

> (*She moves to the door,* OCTAVIUS *meekly accompanies her.*)

DUKE OCTAVIUS All right, my dear. No hurry. Go to bed, sleep on it! See you in the morning.

DUKE FREDERICK My God, are you going to let the Cat's Kitten treat you like that? If I'd my legs . . . Stop her!

DUKE ERNEST She's gone.

> (*She has indeed.* OCTAVIUS *having unlocked the door for her, returns, shamed and crestfallen.*)

DUKE FREDERICK (*explosively*) Why the Hell did you let her out? Call yourself a man!

DUKE OCTAVIUS If I hadn't, I shouldn't be. She'd have p . . .

> (*What she would have done remains unrecorded. Holy Writ comes to the rescue. The Chaplain once more finds himself, on the wrong page.*)

TURNBULL We brought nothing into the world, and it is certain that we can carry nothing out. The Lord gave . . . etc.

> (*His words fall into inaudibility; for now, confusedly and altogether, the Uncles are talking: so much together, that one can hardly hear a word.*)

112

DUKE ERNEST	So you didn't pull it off, Tom, after all.
DUKE OCTAVIUS	What I say is, if I hadn't, she'd have made a dud eunuch of me!
DUKE THOMAS	Damn her! The Kitten's got all the old Cat's claws in one of her little fingers!
DUKE FREDERICK	Call yourselves men, any of you! Call yourselves men! If I could have got hold of her, I'd have put her across my knee and spanked her!

GEORGE AUGUSTUS Where is she? What have you done with her? Who the Hell has taken her?

TURNBULL Since it hath pleased the Lord to take from us this our dear sister departed . . .

DUKE THOMAS Damn it, man! you're drunk. No wonder we couldn't get her to the scratch, when the parson was drunk.

TURNBULL I am not more drunk than your Royal Highness graciously made me.

GEORGE AUGUSTUS Where is she, I say? No one is going to have her if I don't! I'm damned if anyone else shall have her! Where the Hell has she gone to?

DUKE FREDERICK Don't break your heart, lad. She ain't worth it. You didn't bring anything down that time; but first shot don't count. Every one must have a miss once in his life.

GEORGE AUGUSTUS A 'miss.' Call her a 'miss.' I didn't come here to *miss* her. I came to missus her!

(*This causes loud laughter; it is the sort of joke the Uncles can relish.*)

H

DUKE THOMAS So you shall yet. You wait a bit!

GEORGE AUGUSTUS Shan't wait! Not going to wa
Where does she sleep?

DUKE ERNEST With the old Cat.

GEORGE AUGUSTUS I'll missus the old Cat too. Miss
'em both! You told me I was going to have her to-nigh
and I'm going to have her!

DUKE THOMAS Steady, Boy! Steady!

GEORGE AUGUSTUS Where's that 'Kitten' you promise
me?

DUKE THOMAS Gone – given us the slip. Damn her!

GEORGE AUGUSTUS But you promised. You said – yo
said –

DUKE THOMAS Yes, George, damn me! I did. Bu
she's got away, run off. Saw you, and was afraid of you.

GEORGE AUGUSTUS I wasn't afraid of *her*. I'm no
afraid of anybody. Not afraid of the whole damn' lot o
you. I want her! I'm going to have her. I want her! I
you don't bring her here, I'll go and find her for mysel
Break in the door, if you don't bring me a woman. I
you don't let me have a woman to-night, I'll – I'll kil
somebody, kill all of you. I want a woman. Find me
woman!

> (DUKE THOMAS *has rung the bell for his best helper
> and now, in the person of* MR. BUNNY, *hel*
> *arrives. Through the continued uproar o*
> GEORGE AUGUSTUS, *as one well accustomed t*
> *such scenes, he inquires imperturbably fo*
> *further orders.*)

BUNNY Did your Royal Highness ring?

DUKE THOMAS Yes, Bunny, for God's sake get him what he wants, or he'll howl the house down.

BUNNY Beg pardon, your Royal Highness, what is it that His Royal Highness does want?

DUKE THOMAS A woman.

BUNNY Very good, your Royal Highness. If His Royal Highness will only be good enough to wait a minute.

DUKE THOMAS Not more than a minute, Bunny, for God's sake! Hurry, man! Hurry!

(BUNNY *hurries to the rescue of the Royal need.*)

DUKE THOMAS All right, George. Wait a bit! Hold your row! She's coming; she's coming.

GEORGE AUGUSTUS Who? Gussy?

DUKE THOMAS Not Gussy; a woman – one that'll suit you better.

GEORGE AUGUSTUS To marry?

DUKE THOMAS No, George; no marrying this one. Marriage, when you are so young, is a mistake.

GEORGE AUGUSTUS Coming – now? Here?

DUKE THOMAS Yes. Your luck's turned. She's going to make you happy. Come, Brothers all, we'd better clear out of this. The show's over.

(ERNEST *and* OCTAVIUS *collect themselves and stagger out. Behind the screen,* BUNNY *enters, reluctantly accompanied.*)

BUNNY You do as I tell you, Maria, and I'll marry you.

> (*He appears round the screen, and stands ready for orders.*)

DUKE THOMAS Got her?

BUNNY It's all arranged, your Royal Highness.

DUKE THOMAS Then bring her in! Bring her in! And, Bunny – His Royal Highness wants his chair wheeled for him.

> (BUNNY *commandingly gestures to his prospective bride; then, with a rapid change to servility, takes charge of the* DUKE's *chair and wheels him away.*)

DUKE FREDERICK (*as he departs*) Good luck to you, George! Sweet slumber! Pleasant dreams!

> (DUKE THOMAS *lecherously inspects the new arrival, reckons she will do, and is retiring, when he catches sight of* MR. TURNBULL *in collapse on a back seat.*)

DUKE THOMAS Come on, you damned parson; you're not wanted here, *now*! No job; no pension; no nothing! You've made a sticky mess of the whole business. . . . Go to it, George! She's here. You've got her.

> (*The* DUKE, *less drunk than the Chaplain, manœuvres him out through the curtains.* GEORGE AUGUSTUS *turns to inspect the meal which has been provided for him.*)

GEORGE AUGUSTUS So you've come, have you? You the woman they've sent me?

MAID (*tremulously*) Yes, your Royal Highness.

GEORGE AUGUSTUS And you're not going to run away, or any bitch trick of that sort?

MAID No, your Royal Highness.

GEORGE AUGUSTUS Come here! . . . Nearer . . . Nearer.

> (*The* MAID *advances a step or two, then stands shrinking. She covers her face with her hands.* GEORGE AUGUSTUS, *sloughing his enforced virginity, takes her in a drunken embrace.*)

CURTAIN

SCENE IV

It is Sunday morning. The dear old DUCHESS *has come down to breakfast to do honour to her guests; for indeed, in those days, breakfast in bed was either a dissolute habit or an invalid's necessity. A frail, huddled figure, she sits wrapped in a shawl, and with shaking hand herself pours out the tea.*

The breakfast that stands on the table is of an exiguous character — a ladies' breakfast for appetites light and delicate — only eggs and toast. On the sideboard are ham, tongue, and beef, but no one touches them. An automaton in the ducal livery makes parade of service for a while, till, at a word from the DUCHESS, *he retires.*

117

The two DUCHESSES *are already at table, but not* AUGUSTA.

DUCHESS AMELIA I am sorry Augusta is late. The maid who attended on her last night did not come this morning; and she had to wait for mine.

DUCHESS CHARLOTTE Oh, my dear, I'm so sorry! Now what can have happened? I must inquire.

> (*Enter* AUGUSTA, *fresh and serene; she curtsies, and kisses her hostess.*)

AUGUSTA I'm so sorry I'm late, Aunt Charlotte.

DUCHESS CHARLOTTE Don't apologise, my dear, your Mama has told me all about it. It's my fault, not yours. And I hope you slept well, my dear?

AUGUSTA Quite well, thank you.. I always do.

DUCHESS CHARLOTTE That's right! It's nice to see you looking so fresh and rosy. No trouble has come to your young life – not yet.

AUGUSTA Not yet, Aunt Charlotte.

DUCHESS CHARLOTTE (*sentimentally*) Ah, but it will. Health is the great thing, next to happiness. While you have the two together life is easy; but when they separate trouble begins.

DUCHESS AMELIA The best way of keeping them, in my opinion, is a regular life; regular habits, and regular hours. That is how I have always trained her. She goes to bed at ten, she rises at eight.

118

DUCHESS CHARLOTTE That will do, John.

(*Exit* FOOTMAN.)

DUCHESS AMELIA I found her fast asleep when I went up last night.

AUGUSTA No, Mama dear. I wasn't asleep.

DUCHESS AMELIA I spoke to you. You did not answer.

AUGUSTA No. I did not answer.

DUCHESS AMELIA Were you concealing anything, Augusta? Those pearls?

AUGUSTA Yes; I was wearing them, Mama.

DUCHESS CHARLOTTE Just like Fido.

DUCHESS AMELIA Did you wear them in your bath, after what I said?

AUGUSTA No, Mama; I wore them to my bath, and I wore them back from my bath. But I did not wear them *in* my bath.

DUCHESS AMELIA I hope not, indeed!

AUGUSTA But I wore them in bed, last night.

DUCHESS AMELIA You would not have done so, had I known.

AUGUSTA So I thought, Mama.

DUCHESS AMELIA Then, Augusta, you pretended to be asleep to deceive me!

DUCHESS CHARLOTTE Oh, never mind, Amelia! That my pearls have given her so much pleasure gives *me* pleasure also. She is my guest, so she mustn't be scolded.

119

(*The* DUCHESS *has poured out* AUGUSTA'S *tea.*) Sugar, my dear?

AUGUSTA (*hesitatingly*) Oh, please!

DUCHESS AMELIA Augusta is not to have sugar this morning.

DUCHESS CHARLOTTE Oh, but why not?

DUCHESS AMELIA I am not pleased with the way she behaved about those pearls.

DUCHESS CHARLOTTE Oh, but that was last night.

DUCHESS AMELIA I only hear of it this morning.

DUCHESS CHARLOTTE Dear, dear! Well! We live and learn, don't we, my dear? . . . More tea, Amelia?

DUCHESS AMELIA Thank you . . . Augusta must not forget the rules to which I have trained her. She tells me everything.

AUGUSTA Not always, Mama.

DUCHESS AMELIA And when else, pray, was there anything you did not tell me?

AUGUSTA I mean last night, Mama.

DUCHESS AMELIA Quite so. Then let that be a lesson.

AUGUSTA Yes, Mama.

DUCHESS CHARLOTTE Oh, Augusta, my dear, would you not have preferred coffee?

DUCHESS AMELIA Augusta does not have coffee for breakfast.

DUCHESS CHARLOTTE Then would she not have liked it for a change?

120

DUCHESS AMELIA I do not think change is good for Augusta. Coffee once in the day is quite enough for her.

DUCHESS CHARLOTTE Ah, well, she is young; yes. And moderation is good for all of us. And *you* slept well too, I hope, Amelia?

DUCHESS AMELIA I did not sleep as well as I usually do. There were noises.

DUCHESS CHARLOTTE Ah! Did they go on? Just after we had gone up to bed I heard such a disturbance, such a shouting of a man's voice. It sounded as if it was in the house. I rang, and I asked – was anything the matter? And I was told – I am so sorry, my dear, that it disturbed you – that one of the men-servants was having a fit. And you heard it, too?

DUCHESS AMELIA I heard it several times.

DUCHESS CHARLOTTE Oh, then he must have gone on having them. How very unfortunate!

DUCHESS AMELIA I don't think it was a fit, if you ask me.

DUCHESS CHARLOTTE Not? Then . . .?

DUCHESS AMELIA I think it was someone drunk in the house.

DUCHESS CHARLOTTE Oh, Amelia, impossible!

DUCHESS AMELIA Drunkenness is not unknown in this country.

DUCHESS CHARLOTTE Ah, but not here in my house, without my knowing of it.

121

DUCHESS AMELIA Do you know everything that goes on in your house, Duchess?

DUCHESS CHARLOTTE Well, no; not everything, perhaps; but most things – things that ought not to happen, I should know. I should be told.

DUCHESS AMELIA Indeed!

DUCHESS CHARLOTTE Oh yes; I'm very particular about my servants; very old-fashioned, I suppose. They must all come to me with good characters. Some have been with me for twenty years. The maid I sent to attend on you, Augusta, the one who took you to your bath – well, she is a most faithful and trustworthy person. Oh, I would trust her with anything. You found her satisfactory, I hope?

AUGUSTA Oh, quite.

DUCHESS CHARLOTTE Well, she would tell me, if anything were to go wrong. For that is a little weakness of hers; she rather likes to tell tales about the others.

DUCHESS AMELIA A most convenient person to have about you.

DUCHESS CHARLOTTE Well, I don't encourage it; but there it is. And living so much at home as I do now, an orderly household is a great comfort. Let me give you another cup of tea, Augusta. . . . The dear King is not very well, I'm afraid.

DUCHESS AMELIA So I gathered from the Court circular yesterday.

DUCHESS CHARLOTTE He only goes out now in a wheeled chair, they tell me – just for half an hour.

DUCHESS AMELIA A wheeled chair has its advantages. It enables those who are in the last stages of their decay to take the air.

DUCHESS CHARLOTTE Oh, don't say 'in the last stages,' my dear. I have to go in one sometimes myself.

DUCHESS AMELIA I assure your Grace, it was only the King I was thinking of.

DUCHESS CHARLOTTE Yes, we must all think of him — and pray. . . . Have you heard how serious and devoutly religious he has become of late?

DUCHESS AMELIA Indeed! A preparation, I hope.

DUCHESS CHARLOTTE Yes. He says now that he finds God is his only friend.

DUCHESS AMELIA That certainly is an improvement. He used to have others — But he was never very friendly to *me*.

AUGUSTA Uncle James was very kind to me, Mama, when I stayed there.

DUCHESS AMELIA Eat your egg, Augusta.

AUGUSTA I *have* eaten it, Mama.

DUCHESS AMELIA That is not the proper way to answer.

DUCHESS CHARLOTTE Then won't you have another, my dear? — For a treat, as it's Sunday, you know.

AUGUSTA No thank you, Aunt Charlotte.

DUCHESS CHARLOTTE Then a little toast and some jam?

AUGUSTA Thank you, I have had quite enough.

123

DUCHESS CHARLOTTE Well, then, if we have all done, we will send for the dear Chaplain. He always reads prayers to me in here. So much more comfortable. You have not seen our Chaplain yet. Mr. Turnbull is his name.

(While speaking, the DUCHESS *has rung the bell; the* FOOTMAN *enters.)*

Tell Mr. Turnbull that we are ready. And ask Miss Angus to come too. Oh, such a good, excellent man. He has been our Chaplain for years; and the Duke has such a respect for him.

DUCHESS AMELIA And he for the Duke, I hope?

DUCHESS CHARLOTTE Oh, yes; he has a great respect for the Duke, of course; indeed for the whole Family. And we for him.

(Enter MISS ANGUS.*)*

Oh, good morning, Miss Angus. Will you get out the prayer-book, please? Ah, here he is. Good morning, Mr. Turnbull.

TURNBULL Good morning, your Royal Highness.

DUCHESS CHARLOTTE Come and let me present you to Her Royal Highness, the Duchess of Bendigo.

DUCHESS AMELIA How do you do?

(The Chaplain bows as a Chaplain should.)

DUCHESS CHARLOTTE And also to Her Royal Highness, the Princess Augusta.

(The PRINCESS *begins to speak the accepted formula. But scarcely has she opened her lips, when* MR.

TURNBULL, *confronted by the awful apparition of a face that he recognises, descends upon his knees, and utters an abject outcry for mercy.*)

TURNBULL Oh, your Royal Highness, forgive me, pardon me! I had no idea *what* I was doing!

DUCHESS CHARLOTTE Why, what in the world is this? Mr. Turnbull, what has come to you?

TURNBULL Oh, I cannot, I cannot say! Her Royal Highness will explain. I must go!

DUCHESS AMELIA Augusta! Have you met this gentleman before?

AUGUSTA Yes, Mama; I met him when I went to my bath last night.

TURNBULL (*in an agony*) Oh yes, yes. It's true! But I had no idea!

DUCHESS AMELIA Met him?

DUCHESS CHARLOTTE Oh, but he ought not to have been there!

AUGUSTA No, Aunt Charlotte, I think he knows that.

DUCHESS AMELIA (*scandalised*) *In* the bathroom?

AUGUSTA No, Mama; on my way to it. Rise, Mr. Turnbull, do not kneel to *me*. For, I assure you, I have said nothing.

TURNBULL (*rising to a state of salvation*) I'm very much obliged to your Highness, very, very much obliged!

AUGUSTA Say no more, Mr. Turnbull. I am sure you were there only by accident.

125

TURNBULL Oh, I can assure your Royal Highness –
only by accident – a most unfortunate accident – *quite* a
misunderstanding.

DUCHESS CHARLOTTE Well, I hope it won't happen
again. It was most out of place, Mr. Turnbull, for you to
have met the Princess just then.

DUCHESS AMELIA It would never have happened in *my*
house!

TURNBULL Oh, no, of course not; it couldn't!

DUCHESS CHARLOTTE Well, then, I must say I am very
sorry it happened in mine. And now let us have prayers,
Mr. Turnbull. You must excuse me, my dear, I have to
sit; my poor knees. Miss Angus, place the cushions.

DUCHESS AMELIA Augusta, you ought to have told me.

AUGUSTA Yes, Mama.

> (MISS ANGUS *places the cushions. The* DUCHESS *sits,
> the rest of the select congregation descends to
> its knees.*)

TURNBULL Let us pray. Merciful and mighty God,
here, as a Christian family, we assemble and bow before
Thee; once more beseeching Thee (*the curtain begins to
drop*) to pardon all our past offences, to blot out all our
misdoings, to renew in us a right spirit; not to weigh in
just judgment anything that we have done amiss, but to
show mercy and forgiveness. . . .

> (*His voice drones on; the Curtain closes.*)